The Alcohol-Woman:

A Powerful 9-Point Plan for Quitting Drinking.

By

Antonia Ryan

Edited by Lewis David
WinsPress.com

About Me.

Many books are out there written by women who have struggled with alcohol during their lives and found solutions that work for them. These autobiographical accounts are inspiring and can incentivize women to get well and stay well. But what helps one person may not be helpful to another. Our values, backgrounds, and personalities are different.

I have experienced a vast range of issues and situations that many women face, and I am at a stage of life where I have a wealth of personal experience to draw on. But I don't just rely on this. In writing this book, I have interviewed dozens of women who have candidly shared their struggles and wisdom with me. I have also been involved in the world of recovery for twenty-five years and have met thousands of women and men who have wrestled with alcohol dependence. This personal involvement has impacted me profoundly.

In recent years I have worked closely at WinsPress.com with Lewis David, my editor. He is a remarkable therapist who has helped thousands to beat the hold of booze over their lives with his bestselling books, including *The 10 Day Alcohol Detox Plan* and *Alcohol and You*. Together we co-authored *Mindfulness for Alcohol Recovery*, which has helped a multitude of readers and listeners to achieve and maintain long-term sobriety.

I also host *The Alcohol Recovery Show*, a podcast to support and inspire anyone interested in recovery. Many listeners have shared their experiences, which have all helped give me a more rounded perspective in approaching writing this book. (You can find information on all the above on Winspress.com.)

My professional background is that of a qualified teacher and social worker. These roles have given me the privilege of working alongside people dealing with issues such as anxiety and substance misuse. I have counseled people with compulsive behavioral issues, providing one-to-one support and guidance.

I also trained and qualified as a meditation and yoga teacher to augment my practice in these professional roles. I have used these modalities to support people in finding ways to self-soothe and release themselves from crippling anxiety, compulsive behaviors, low moods, and exhaustion.

In this book, I talk about the issues many women face in our modern culture. As a working mother with a family and a home to run, I can relate to the exhaustion and overwhelm many women report feeling. I get it. Uncorking that bottle of wine and blotting out the fatigue doesn't seem optional – it's a way of coping.

Lastly, I come from a background in which heavy drinking was endemic. I grew up in Ireland. Half of my family was teetotal, but the other half most definitely was not. The teetotallers tutted and shook their heads at the drinkers, and there was a lot of shame around any whiff of a drinking problem.

Looking back as an adult, I see that many of my neighbors and my friends' parents had issues with drinking. Doors were closed firmly and curtains were drawn. It just wasn't discussed. As a teenager, the message I was given was that the only thing worse than a drunk man was a drunk woman. A drunk man was excused as blowing off steam or relaxing. A drunk woman was a source of whispered gossip and pitying glances. It was a secret, shameful thing. I have lived through changing times.

So this book is a synthesis of personal experience, active recovery, and professional training and practice. Most importantly, I present a structured 9-point plan that will walk you through that life free from alcohol dependence. My profound hope is that the precepts in the book are actionable, engaging, comforting, and supportive and will take you to a life free from alcohol dependence.

Before We Get Started.

Healthcare workers and alcohol treatment professionals use a questionnaire called AUDIT, which stands for Alcohol Use Disorders Identification Test. This gives an instant assessment how severe (or otherwise) a person's alcohol use is. It's not complicated to use: the drinker simply answers 10 questions, and they get a score.

Before you get into my program, I suggest you find out what your AUDIT score is, as it gives you a start point, and it will give you feedback on the seriousness of your alcohol use. If you have never done this before, I'm sure you are curious to know, so I'm going to show you how to do it right now. There are three steps:

Step One.

You will need a copy of the questionnaire. Because it isn't suitable to reproduce in an e-book (it would appear too small to read on your device) I have a PDF version for you to download, and you can print this off if you wish.

To get the PDF, go to subscribepage.com/auditquiz. A copy of AUDIT will be emailed to you. If you cannot see it in your email inbox after a couple of minutes, check folders like "spam" or "promotions" in case it hasn't gone to your main inbox. If you still can't find it, click this alternative link: https://tinyurl.com/yxddcfck

Step Two.

Before you answer the questions on your copy of AUDIT, you will need to work out how many units of alcohol you consume on a typical drinking day. This isn't complicated. Across the top of the questionnaire, you will see examples of units of alcohol. For example, you will see that one measure of a spirit (which is about the amount that you would need to fill the bottle's cap) is about one unit, a bottle of wine is about 9 units, a pint of regular beer is 2 units, and so on.

You should be able to work out roughly how many units you drink in a day. It doesn't have to be exact. If you are having any difficulty working out your units, try using the online calculator at https://tinyurl.com/yy4hlaze.

Step Three.
Now it's time to answer the 10 questions. For each question, you will score between $0 - 4$, depending on your answer.

You must answer all 10 questions. If you leave any blank, it will screw up the results. If none of the answers seems right for you, choose the one which sounds nearest to a correct reply. And choose only one answer for each of the 10 questions, so you should have a score of 0, 1, 2, 3, or 4 for each one.

When you have finished, total up your scores. The maximum score possible is 40.

What your score tells you.
A score of $0 - 7$. You are a light-to-moderate drinker. Although there is no safe level for alcohol consumption except zero, you are at low risk.

A score of 8 – 15. You are an increasing-risk drinker. You would be advised to decrease or stop your drinking.

A score of 16 – 19. You are a higher-risk drinker. You are getting into the danger zone.

A score of 20 – 40. At this level, you might be alcohol-dependent, and the higher your score over 20, the more harm alcohol is doing to you. You should consider seeking medical support as well as reading this book.

Now you know your starting point. But whatever your score, don't despair, because this book is going to help you turn around your drinking issues – once and for all.

So let's get started.

Table Of Contents

PART ONE.

There Are No 'Shoulds'.

There are no 'shoulds' in this book, but there are plenty of 'coulds'. All the ideas, hints, tools, and perspectives are presented as a toolbox for you to dip into and pull out what you need at a particular stage in your life or recovery journey. I intend this book to be read by anyone interested in living a life free from any form of alcohol dependence, whether they are curious about a booze-free lifestyle or have been sober for years and just need some motivation to keep going.

I do not write this book from any vantage point of moral authority – simply as a woman who has experienced the issues many of my readers might face. We live in an advice epidemic. Now more than ever, myriad voices tell us how to live, what to eat, how to optimize, and how to be 'the best version of ourselves'. But I am not telling you what to do. I make suggestions. So take what applies to you.

If a suggestion does not resonate with you, don't do it. This doesn't mean anything is wrong with you. This is *your* recovery, no one else's. It can be tempting to hand responsibility to the advisor because if it doesn't work out, you can point the finger of blame at the advisor. So instead, with a sense of personal responsibility, choose the tools and tips that you think will work for you.

I write these words for women who lead real lives, with families and jobs; who worry about their elderly parents or their teenage kids; who struggle to keep up with helping the kids with their homework and paying the mortgage. For many of us, time or money is just not available for therapy, yoga classes, massages, spa days, or meditation classes. If these activities help you, then go ahead and build them into your recovery. But I am acknowledging that not everyone can or wants to pursue activities that are often touted as *the* way to get sober. You can get sober in a way that suits you – your tastes, personality, time, and budget. And, you do not have to take out a second mortgage to do it.

There are plenty of suggestions to get started and keep going on a life of recovery from alcohol dependence. A quick fix doesn't usually last. You might think you have a drinking problem, but the drinking problem is just a symptom. By working out for yourself what it is a symptom of, you can start to get to the root of the issue. Superficial mind hacks, life hacks, or tips might help for a while, but going a little deeper will help build a strong, sustainable, and solid recovery from alcohol dependence.

Reliance on alcohol does not happen in a vacuum. This dependence, including psychological dependence, is very much a product of our experiences. By broadening our understanding of all issues, we can make empowered choices to build and maintain recovery.

The Plan.

If drinking has caused you problems and you have found it hard to stop, you need a plan. Sobriety will not happen by magic and it certainly won't be sustainable without a plan.

Imagine I sent you out to navigate your way through a minefield. A mine could blow up in your face at any moment. Wouldn't you rather know where the mines are so you can move through them safely? Would you feel safer if you had a map in your hand of where the mines are located? You can then work out a route through the minefield.

Look on the plan in this book as your route map through to being alcohol-free. The plan can keep you safe, help you avoid relapse, and teach you the skills you need to find your way through early recovery and beyond.

Most advice is gender-neutral, not meeting our specific needs as women. I spoke or interacted with hundreds of women in my research for this book and found that for many of them, their roles as females in society had influenced how they approached drinking and responded to life's challenges.

This book goes deeper than many 'how to stop drinking' books. It addresses the thoughts, attitudes, and actions that have created the problem to begin with, and how to change those thoughts, attitudes, and actions to create an alcohol-free life. Recovery is a psychological journey, so you will need psychological tools. I examined these from a female perspective, so this book has a plan that is perfect for you as a woman who wishes to be alcohol-free.

Having been involved in recovery for nearly 25 years, I have experience in many recovery programs. I used this knowledge to inform the plan I put forward in this book.

The plan is holistic. That means all the different parts of it work together to help get you well and stay that way.

I want you to start The 9-Point Plan as soon as possible. I begin with actions to do as soon as you begin reading about the details of The Plan. Briefly, the 9 points of The Plan are:

1. Have a plan. The chances of relapsing are high without a plan.

2. Follow the plan every day, especially when you don't feel like it. That's when you need it most.

3. Treat yourself well. Be kind to your body and mind.

4. Absorb uplifting books or audio content to keep you motivated. Read, listen, or watch every day.

5. Self-reflect and grow. Learn new skills and develop new attitudes. Be open to change.

6 Enjoy an activity you like as a reward every day. Play and take pleasure in life.

7. Talk to a trusted friend or friends.

8. Be aware of your thinking around triggers to drink and learn strategies to deal with them.

9. Deal with disturbing emotions, whether these are from your past, present, or worries about the future.

I will explain what to do and how to do it. But first off, let's be clear about *why* you are doing it. We will look at that next.

Find Your 'Why'.

There are lots of 'how-to' books, but if you don't know *why* you are doing something, then *how* is irrelevant. So, I want you to get specific and think about your purpose.

I'm not talking about your big life purpose. That's way too hard to work out at this stage. Later, when your head has cleared and you get to know yourself better, the bigger picture will get easier to see and you can move on to your life purpose then. But right now, I am talking about your purpose in getting sober.

If you are already clear about your reasons for stopping and feel very motivated, that's brilliant news. But I would urge you to read this section anyway, even if you feel you are keen to get started.

Alternatively, you might know that you *should* stop drinking. You know deep down that it is causing you problems, but you just can't get started. Perhaps you feel stuck in a cycle of drinking, regret, repeat. You might be a daily drinker, but although you function, you often feel lousy. You go to work or look after the kids, but what keeps you going is the thought of a drink at the end of the day. A drink is your 'reward,' and you feel sad at the thought of losing this special treat. Maybe you want to feel less lethargic, depressed, sad, or stressed, and you know that drinking isn't helping. But you can't break out of the trap.

No one is keeping you in the trap. The trap is your thinking. Your thinking directs your actions, and your actions are getting you into trouble. This could be health trouble, problems with the law, issues with loved ones, or difficulties at work. Perhaps the trap feels like a grim Groundhog Day existence. Every day feels the same and you want to break out of it – but can't seem to muster the willpower.

Getting out of the funk of routine heavy drinking is difficult without help. You might know with your intellect that you 'should' stop. You probably realize already heavy drinking is not doing your health, looks, career, family, or bank balance much good. But you just can't find the motivation to stop.

However, you have had the motivation and willpower to get this book. You have made a start. The hard bit is over. Motivation and willpower have done their job. It's like tipping the first domino in a long line of dominoes. Once the first domino goes down, they all tumble in a row. By following the plan and absorbing the ideas in this book, you will breeze through the first few days of sobriety. Do the actions, take in the ideas, and sobriety will happen. So just relax.

It's natural to feel anxious about the thought of not drinking. After all, you may well have started drinking to deal with nervousness or emotional discomfort. If you are a regular, heavy drinker, your body will go into mild withdrawal when you stop, and you will feel out of sorts for a short time. As a drink would get rid of the withdrawal, no wonder it is difficult to stop. But that soon passes.

Alcohol may well be your solution for social awkwardness or anxiety. You might use it to pick yourself up when you feel low or to calm yourself down when you feel wired. Perhaps routines such as uncorking a bottle of wine when you get home from work or pouring a gin and tonic as you cook dinner are woven into the fabric of your daily life. If you are not a daily drinker, perhaps you binge on a weekend. You know you need to cut down or stop but can't let go of the excitement of the big night out on a Friday or Saturday. You might rebel against anyone who suggests you cut down and feel they are controlling you.

Alternatively, you might want to stop drinking and be able to do so, but the problem is that the booze lures you back in again after a few days, weeks, or months. You just can't stay stopped, even though you want to. However, this book will provide you with all the support and strategies you need to stop.

Maybe you already have some serious motivation. It could be a DUI or the threat of losing your driving license. Or it could be an ultimatum from a loved one, a health scare, or the latest embarrassing drunken episode that has just gone too far. Maybe you have worries about losing your spouse or your children because of your drinking. Even if they stay in your life, losing their respect and trust is ongoing agony.

This form of motivation might work short-term if you want to save a marriage, heal from an illness, or repair your reputation. But will it work long-term? Alcohol has been your crutch, your best friend. You fear losing alcohol almost as much as you fear losing your family, your home, or your job. You want to avoid the negative consequences of drinking, but you also want to avoid *not* drinking.

You are at a crossroads: you can't carry on as you are, but you can't face life without alcohol. This can feel like a very dark and fearful place. You might feel you are stuck with an impossible choice because it seems like either way you lose. I get that, and that's why I am suggesting to you that you consider what you will get from not drinking.

If you're not sure, let me share with you what you will get from not drinking. This is based on my experience and that of countless readers of my books, listeners to my podcast, clients, and friends. None of us is any better than you. We all have been in that same agonizing dilemma of knowing we can't carry on drinking but being too frightened, depressed, or unwilling to stop. But read on because below I list some of the good stuff you get when you stop and stay stopped. I am not trying to convince you, but I would be selling you short if I didn't run you through a list of some of the great things that just happen naturally when you put the cork back in the bottle.

First, sleep – no more waking up at 4 a.m. with a raging thirst and a racing heart. Second, energy, bags of energy. Third, mental sharpness and quicker reaction times. Next, self-respect and the renewed trust of other people. Shall I go on? There's more. You get an improved appearance, glowing skin, clearer eyes, an attractive physique, and feeling fitter and more energetic. You will want to move more and perhaps take up sports or physical pastimes you avoided when drinking.

And there's more. You will most likely feel calmer, less anxious, and not so easily roused to anger. You will have the mental energy to want to learn and grow. And this is one I love: you will get peace of mind. You won't need to worry in the morning after the night before about what you said or did when drunk. You will have the freedom to drive where you want and when you want, without having to work around your drinking or face legal consequences. You will get to keep your purse, phone, and keys when you go out in the evening (a friend of mine even lost her shoes on numerous occasions when out drinking – it hasn't happened once since she stopped). You will get your self-esteem and your pride in yourself back.

The list could go on, but I will end it here with a reminder that you will also get the most precious commodity we have – time. All that time spent in a blackout, sleeping off the drink, recovering from a drinking spree, and feeling rough is all the quality time you get back. It's *quality* time because you feel well, energetic, and calm enough to do rewarding things, which ultimately makes you a more dynamic, and engaging person.

If you have been drinking heavily for a long period, you might need to talk with your doctor or at least cut down gradually. You have probably heard about the dangers of stopping heavy drinking suddenly. You can still read this book and cut back a little each day. I would suggest cutting out one drink each day until you are down to zero.

But if you are in any doubt at all, speak with a medical practitioner.

Above all, if you decide to cut down and stop, give the process some time. Although there are no guarantees, if you give the process time and bring to it an open mind and a willingness, you will start to experience some of the good stuff I have listed above.

You can make an informed choice about your drinking. I am not telling you what to do. If you are deciding to do something about your drinking because you want to, you will be making a positive choice *for yourself.* This might be to make your life bigger and more vibrant.

And after all, every time you are offered a drink or have an opportunity to buy it or consume it, *you* will need to make a choice – will you have a drink or not? It is so much easier to make that choice because you positively want to be sober. Making the choice is easy because you understand what has been going on, and you see the bigger picture. It's not just about avoiding being embarrassed, or ill, alone, broke, homeless, or risking jail or some other institution. You are not making your choice based on fear or to placate a partner or loved one.

You are doing it for *yourself.*

Your relationships, money situation, career, and health will improve when you stop drinking at unsafe levels. But your life still might not be perfect. Your marriage might break up, your finances might take a nosedive, or you might lose your job. Sadly, these things happen in most people's lives at some stage. But if life hits a rocky patch, at least you will be sober. And if you are sober, you have a fighting chance of dealing with a setback more effectively. This will ensure the best outcomes for yourself, and others affected.

So instead of focusing on what you want to *avoid losing* by not drinking, think about what you will *get* from being alcohol-free. You might want better relationships or to be a more effective employee or to feel more vibrant and energetic. You might want to look your best and age well.

As women, many of us are conditioned to take care of and nurture others. A shift in focus from worrying about losing or hurting others to working out what we want for ourselves can feel uncomfortable. It can seem selfish. But, even if does feel selfish or uncomfortable, set aside any shame or fear and take a few moments to consider positive reasons why you want to get sober *for yourself.*

This is important. The reason you want to get sober is *your purpose*. So take some time to think this one through. We will come back to it. I can't tell you what your purpose in getting sober is.

Alcohol might give us a false sense of freedom or release, a temporary 'high' (research indicates that this high lasts for about twenty minutes and it's all downhill from there). But these empty promises touted by advertisers and 'big alcohol' is an illusion because alcohol takes much more than it gives.

Think about what alcohol has taken from you: your self-esteem, your pride, your peace of mind, your energy, your mental acuity. It might already have taken your children, home, or driving license. All this for twenty minutes or less of a jolly feeling.

It's not much of a trade-off, is it?

The responsibilities modern society puts on us might make us feel overwhelmed, and alcohol is promoted as a magic elixir that gives us freedom. But, in effect, we have been swindled into drinking. It's not a conspiracy. It's just business. But the result is that advertisers and an alcohol-obsessed culture have brainwashed us. (There is more on this in the last section of the book). What alcohol is doing is dumbing us down. It's dumbing down our voice, our creativity, our energy, and our self-respect. And rather than giving us freedom, it is constraining us in a life that just gets smaller and smaller.

You might feel you already have a big dollop of shame plopped onto your head, so you might feel apologetic and humble. Perhaps you have tried a well-known non-drinking program and been told you *should* be humbler. Maybe you have even been told your ego needs to be crushed. This can feel harsh and confusing.

Some of us might have egos that are bolstered by taking care of others and built up by being caring mothers, loving wives, or attentive daughters. Our egos might have already been eroded by abuse or trauma or a deep sense of being 'less than' so we run around after others to strengthen the ego.

But instead of thinking continually of others to bolster the ego, we need to connect with others *and* ourselves. This is not selfish. It is psychologically healthy, and you have a right to that. You have a right to work out what is going to work for you. This is what you are doing right now, and it is important. You are connecting with yourself and working out your purpose. Getting this right will help you. In turn, it will be helpful to all the people in your life who want to see you happy and sober. So, imagine them all cheering you on and smiling.

Take these next few minutes to think hard about your purpose for getting sober. When you have done that, make a note of it. Jot it onto a note app on your phone or into a diary. You could open a file on your PC or set up a secret board on Pinterest. Whatever works for you. The important thing is to record your purpose for getting sober.

Later in this part of the book, we will re-visit this exercise to refine your ideas, but for now, write down the thoughts that come to mind regarding your reasons for wanting to be alcohol-free. This is your first exercise as a foundation for the plan.

So now that you are clearer about your *why,* let's get on to *what* you need to do in the next chapter.

What to Do.

I start with actions because anyone can change their actions right away. Today.

Our actions and behavior are where we can make progress quickly because we can see what they are easily. So, let's start with the easy stuff and work from there.

The first two points of the plan. are to:

1. Have a plan. A simple, structured plan makes getting through early sobriety easy. We discussed this in detail in the chapter called 'The Plan.'
2. Follow it every day. The Plan has activities you do every day to stay healthy and well. To remain alcohol-free, you will need to do some things each day to make sure you stay that way, so the plan needs to be followed each day. I will explain the details of this in the section coming up.

This is *what* you need to do every day as part of that structure and routine:

Look after your body.

I'm sure you know that drinking enough water, sufficient sleep, getting some exercise, fresh air, and eating your veggies make you feel better. I'm not going to patronize or bore you by preaching about it. But if you are not doing those things, the following is my go-to when I get into a slump. I call it *Feel Great in Eight*.

I sleep for 8 hours and walk for 8,000 steps (if you cannot walk, stretch for 8 minutes outside). I eat 8 portions of fruit and vegetables per day, drink 8 glasses of water, sit down and do nothing except breathe (no phone, no TV, no talking) for 8 minutes at least once each day. These are the basics, so start there. Make a list (sleep, move, fruit/veg, water, relax), and tick off these five basics of sound health if you need to.

Although you may feel all fired up and inspired to have a healthy lifestyle, now is *not* the time for going cold turkey on caffeine and sugar. If you smoke, it will of course be better to aim to stop at some point but not in the first few days or weeks of stopping drinking. Take it easy. Concentrate on staying alcohol-free and cut back gradually on caffeine, sugar, or, nicotine. If you go full-throttle trying to give up everything at once, it's going to be too much.

Read and Listen.

Read positive stuff related to recovery. What goes into our brains shapes our thinking and behavior. Books have changed my life and they can change yours too, a day at a time. So read something to help you stay sober every day.

To get started, read some of this book every day. If you read a chapter each day, that would take you through one full month of sobriety. A fantastic start.

If you prefer listening to reading, you could listen to a podcast or audiobook every day that makes you feel upbeat and motivated to stay sober. People have found my podcast, *The Alcohol Recovery Show*, which I host with Lewis David, to be helpful. You can find the podcast, which is free, at WinsPress.com/podcast. (You can find other free resources on the WinsPress.com website under the 'Free Stuff' tab.) This book is also available as an audiobook.

Take an idea or a sentence from what you read and keep it in mind for that day. It could be a quality you want to grow in your character, or it could be an affirmation, a short prayer, or a tip for staying sober. Whatever resonates with you. Ideally, read or listen first thing in the morning. It will help set you up for the day. But if you forget, just do it as soon as you remember. Don't think, ''I've missed my opportunity now. I'll just do it tomorrow''.

Don't wait, do it as soon as you can.

Check in with at least one sober friend or mentor.

This is someone you can be honest and open with: the type of friend who will call you out if you are making excuses or being evasive. By 'checking in' I mean a phone call, video call, or face-to-face meeting. If you have a Facebook friend who knows your story and can relate to you and support you, connect with them. If you have a sponsor or therapist or recovery coach, talk to them.

Talk to them even when you don't know what to say. Tell them how you are feeling that day and what is going on for you. If you have nothing to say, tell them you are just checking in with them and you have nothing much to report. That's okay. It's making the effort to show up that counts.

There is no point in having a sponsor or therapist if you don't use them. You know, like a trophy you keep on your mantelpiece from a school sports performance. It looks nice, but you don't use it for anything. The trophy just sits there for show. So, engage with your support person. If you outgrow them, find someone else.

If you already attend a recovery group, keep this up. If you have found a group helpful, keep attending – don't try to go it alone.

If you don't have anyone who you can talk to openly, spend some time today finding people who are sober and well. Join some online groups or follow up on any suggestions or contacts you might have from a doctor or recovery counselor you are working with. I have included some suggestions for groups in the resource section of this book.

Do something that lights you up (that doesn't involve alcohol).

Do something that puts you into 'the zone'. You know – when time just flies by because you are so absorbed in an activity you love to do. If you don't know what it is, think about what you used to enjoy or what you liked to do as a child. For some people, it could be nature. It could be as simple as spending some time outdoors walking and enjoying the feel of the breeze and the sights and sounds around you. For others, spiritual practice or a sport might be the answer.

But do something that gives you a sense of enjoyment, that makes life feel like it is worth living. It doesn't matter what it is – a hobby, sport, craft, physical activity, a musical skill, or DIY. But do one thing every day that you love to do. Ideally, write down a list of all the things you used to enjoy doing or things you want to do but were too tired, too hungover, or too drunk to do before.

Doing something you enjoy eliminates many problems people meet in early recovery. People complain about having too much time on their hands. Don't see this as a problem. See it as an opportunity to do all the stuff you never had time to do before. Boredom is often mentioned as an issue, so doing fun stuff overcomes this. Use your activity as a reward for being sober. I have found that people who build in a reward are successful at maintaining their alcohol-free lifestyle, so do something you enjoy as a treat to keep you motivated.

Self-reflection and growth.

Go back over your recent actions. This means thinking about your behavior, especially in situations you have found difficult. Ask yourself if there is anything you would do differently. This is self-reflection.

Looking at your behavior might feel a bit weird at first if you are not used to doing it. Alcohol will have made things fuzzy, so looking at yourself in this way can seem strange but necessary. Bear with me on this.

Let's use the analogy of a home. When you think about it, your body and mind are a type of home for yourself that goes everywhere with you. If it is tidy, clean, and comfortable, it is a good place to be. If it needs some attention – perhaps things are lurking about in the corners that are a bit icky – you won't feel happy there.

By looking at your actions, you are keeping your body and mind in good repair. It might feel hard at first, but it will get easier. If you find it difficult, you can ask your sober friend, mentor, sponsor, or counselor to help you. You can talk through your behavior with them and work out better ways to deal with life.

Self-reflection is a skill that helps you be aware of the feelings that come up for you in response to certain people, places, or events. These feelings could trigger a drink, so self-reflection is an important skill to keep you sober.

When you are reflecting on your actions, thoughts, or responses, be kind towards yourself. It is not an exercise in some sort of self-punishment. It is to help you learn and move forward. Be gentle with yourself and give some slack. Life can be hard. Don't make it harder. See what it is you have done, note it, and think of a better way to do it next time.

Self-reflection and self-awareness are key aspects of growth. Growth means getting better at handling difficult experiences in life. It means growing skills so that we can get on better with other people and feel happier in ourselves. If we are not growing and moving forward, we are stuck. Stagnation leaves room to slip back into old patterns, back into outmoded, unconscious behavior that could lead right back to a drink, so keep moving forward.

By engaging in regular, daily self-reflection, it is easier to catch ourselves slipping back into old patterns before they become re-established as a habit.

There will be lots of easy exercises to try out as part of your daily self-reflection, so keep reading. Also, there is a summary of the most significant exercises in the appendix at the back of the book to use as a quick reference. Using these strategies will help keep you sober and content and are a good way to track your growth.

So, today, and every day, this is a summary of what to do:

- Look after your body.
- Spend a few moments on self-reflection. Think about your actions and reactions.
- Do something you enjoy and build in a little reward for being sober that day.
- Read or listen to some literature to keep you motivated to stay alcohol-free. Keep reading this book every day as a starter. Keep re-reading it if needed.
- Talk to a friend who wants to help you stay alcohol-free and is willing to be honest with you.

Remember, the key to success is doing these actions every day. So, to help you remember I have created a memory aid to bring the five points to mind, the word is:

TREAT

1. **T**reat your body well
2. **R**eflect on your actions
3. **E**njoy an activity
4. **A**bsorb uplifting content
5. **T**alk to a trusted friend

So, begin today to TREAT yourself well. Do these actions today and every day to help you stay alcohol-free.

On a bad day when you are struggling with cravings or feel overwhelmed, just remember the word TREAT. Treat your body well, reflect on how you are feeling and what is going on for you, do something you enjoy, absorb some uplifting content and talk to someone. You can do those things over the space of 24 hours.

You have learned about the first two points of the plan, in the next chapter, we will go on to the third point:

Point 3: **Have structure and routine.** Having a routine ensures the actions you take to stay alcohol-free become habitual. When activities are habitual, you need less effort, willpower, and motivation, so habits make staying alcohol-free easier. In the next section, I talk about the power of following a routine. Later, I cover other key ideas such as managing craving thoughts and triggers and dealing with bad moods. So, keep reading to deal with these common problems in early recovery.

Summary

- Points one and two of the plan are to have a plan to do it every day.
- The basic actions of the plan can be summarized as a memory aid: *TREAT*
- TREAT stands for: *Treat* your body well. *Reflect* on your actions, thoughts, and feelings. *Enjoy* an activity. *Absorb* inspiring content. *Talk* to a trusted friend or mentor.

When to Do It.

Maybe you are like me and you hate routine. I balk at the idea of doing the same thing at the same time every day. Some people love a routine. It makes them feel safe. But for me, even the word 'routine' makes me feel a bit deflated. So how do you establish a routine even if you despise them?

Whether you love them or loathe them, we all have routines. All of us fall into routine behavior and reactions unless we are very self-aware. Our routine behavior is often on a type of default setting or autopilot – that type of mental zone you go into when you have driven home from work, but you can't remember the actual details of the journey. You were sober and awake, but the specific memory is blank. That's autopilot.

The antidote to autopilot is awareness. Awareness shakes us out of that autopilot. Reviewing our routines under the spotlight of awareness ensures we are living life with intention and purpose, not just cruising along thoughtlessly. So reviewing your routine will help avoid slipping into default mode – and the routines that lead us to drink.

For example, an old routine might have been to go straight to the grocery store after work and buy wine. Even if you don't intend to buy wine, it somehow ends up in your shopping cart. This is an example of a routine that needs to be replaced with a new one. We want to replace these old routines with *better* routines.

Establishing helpful routines helps avoid reacting to old triggers, such as the shopping trigger above. The trigger could also be an emotional one. Something upsets you, so you become angry, shout and rage irrationally, then feel awful and drink. This chain of events is an old pattern.

Instead of reacting in an old routine manner, we need to develop new skills in responding to emotional triggers. Tiresome people and difficult situations, for instance, trigger the urge to drink for many people. But these challenges are part of life, and we need to deal with them without getting overly upset and reaching for a drink.

Many suggestions in this book concern looking at patterns of thinking and behavior and replacing them with more helpful patterns. This makes controlling your drinking simpler because if you defuse the *trigger* to drink, you won't get the *urge* to drink. That's a whole lot easier than having to use willpower to deal with urges.

Having an established plan of action and *helpful* routines means you will manage triggers without acting out or getting drunk. People can be unreasonable and dreadful things can happen. Life will seem unfair at times. Having your planned activities keeps you healthy and motivated to stay alcohol-free because those triggers have less of an effect on you.

In the last chapter, I introduced the 5 daily actions to help get you sober and keep you sober. You will remember the memory aid: TREAT. The 5 actions are:

- **T**reat your body well
- **R**eflect

- **E**njoy an activity you like as a reward every day
- **A**bsorb uplifting books or audio content to keep you motivated
- **T**alk to a trusted friend

The following is a story about a woman named Marianne. Her experiences illustrate why new actions and routines to support being alcohol-free are needed. It's not enough to just stop drinking and keep your fingers crossed.

Marianne had managed to stay sober for two months but drank again. She contacted me to try to figure out what happened. She explained that previously she had been drinking two bottles of wine each day. She had stopped this after being told by her doctor that her liver was in bad shape. After a few tricky days of feeling shaky and sick, her head had cleared, and she felt better than she had done in years. Marianne was amazed at the amount of energy she had and was doing well at work and getting jobs done at home.

However, Marianne still had the same routines, the same job, the same friends, and went to the same places, except she didn't drink. She still sat up late at night but drank cola instead of wine and went to the pub with her friends on a Friday night. Marianne didn't know anyone else who didn't drink. Out of the blue, she had a big bust-up with her partner. He walked out and Marianne did what she always did when she was upset and angry – she drank wine.

The problem was that Marianne had not changed her routine. She did all the same things but without alcohol. She had not developed any skills to cope with life's challenges such as relationship problems. For a while, she had felt well but had taken this for granted. When she drank again, it was as if she had forgotten all the problems it had caused before.

Marianne did the 5 actions I suggest. She took better care of herself physically, read some 'quit-lit' every day, rang her mentor for a quick chat, and spent a few minutes reflecting on her day each evening. Instead of going to the pub, she went to a Pilates class with a friend from work. She built a life that involved a variety of activities. In addition, Marianne put thought into what she would do instead of drinking if she were upset. She changed her daily actions.

To make sure the actions happen for you, you could peg the action onto something you want to do. For example, if you love coffee, read your recovery literature first thing in the morning as you drink that essential first cup. If you look forward to a long hot shower or soak in the bath, use this time to reflect on how you have handled your day.

The daily actions do not have to be done in Instagram-worthy settings or circumstances. It is much better to do the action imperfectly, even if the circumstances or surroundings are not exactly right. For example, if you have had a tough day at work, reflecting on it during your bathroom time is effective. Having a lovely meditation room is great, but never using it is a waste of time. So don't stress about the perfect environment to self-reflect – just get on with it wherever you can.

When thinking about a new routine, start small and short. It's easy to get fired up by a new regime, but don't overcommit. It's much better to do a little than nothing at all. They say the road to hell is paved with good intentions. I don't know about hell, but the road to disappointment and lack of results is paved with good intentions that never turn into consistent action. So just do it.

Whether or not you like having a routine, review it regularly. I find it helps to shake things up every three months. Seasons change, life happens, and I change up my routine to accommodate my need for novelty and the changing season. But I do the five actions in some form. In summer I might sit outside and read inspiring literature first thing in the morning and have a walk later in the day to spend some time self-reflecting. In winter, these actions will be based more indoors or somewhere cozy. When I had children at home, or when I did jobs that had unsocial hours, my routines were different. Build a routine with the five actions that work for you, now.

'Okay, I get the idea' you might think. But will you do it? I have spoken to loads of people who have struggled in the first few days and weeks of sobriety. It is like they have expected a new way of living their lives to just happen. In the early days, you will need to put in a little effort to ensure things go smoothly. To give yourself a fighting chance to overcome triggers and establish a new way of living, I am going to ask you to get organized. This will mean thinking about how you will build the five actions called **TREAT**, which we were just discussing.

You will need to build these into your daily routine in a very practical way.

So, before you finish this chapter, I am going to ask you to complete your very own *'TREAT Schedule'* open a word app or computer file and create a timetable with 8 columns and 6 rows. If you are using a pen and paper draw 9 lines going down and 7 lines across to create a schedule. Across the top line write in the name of each day, Monday to Sunday, and down the side write 'T' in the second box down, then 'R' in the next one, followed by 'E,' then 'A' in the fifth box and 'T' in the sixth box. You will remember these letters stood for these headings that made up the word: TREAT. Now, you will be thinking and planning the where, when, what, and who will be involved. You are thinking about the exact practicalities. If you don't plan and write it down, it probably won't happen. So, do it now.

For example:

'T,' (Treat your body well): You could note down that you will take a ten-minute walk at 7.30 am around your local park. Make a note of wake-up and bedtimes, mealtimes, and movement time for a pedicure, massage, or haircut. Once a week or so, you could book a massage or special treat, using the money you save on booze.

'R,' (Reflect): You will spend some time in self-reflection at 9.30 pm as you prepare for bed.

'E' (Enjoy an activity as a reward): This will depend on what fires you up, but for example, it could be spending one-hour gardening on Monday, one-hour painting on Tuesday, 30 minutes on jewelry making on Wednesday, and so on.

'A' (Absorb uplifting content): This might be the same most days for a period and then change. For example, read one chapter of this book. After a month or so, you might change to a different book or listen to a podcast such as *The Alcohol Recovery Show.*' But to get you into the routine, jot down what you will absorb to keep you motivated and on track.

'T' (Talk to a friend): Note down who you will speak with, the time you intend to talk with them, and how – will you ring them or see them in person?

Think about the practical considerations: *When* will you do it? *Where* will you do it and *what* will you use?

Be as specific as you can. Note timeframes if needed. For example, spend at least ten minutes in self-reflection.

Establishing a routine is the best way to ensure your recovery actions happen, so put some thought into your day-to-day routines. Design a routine that you know you can stick to easily. At first, this might seem a bit clunky, but it will get easier. Sticking to your routine will make consistency effortless. It is consistency, doing the actions daily, that gets results and works in the long term.

It won't feel like a big, special effort to carry out actions to stay well, because the daily actions become part of the fabric of your daily life like brushing your teeth or drinking water.

In these first chapters, we have covered the basic stuff: the actions. These actions are the day-to-day framework. As the book progresses, we will go deeper to uncover thinking and ideas that could sabotage your non-drinking.

Keep doing the actions as you continue to read and apply what I suggest in the rest of the book. This is just the beginning.

As I mentioned earlier, triggers – like troublesome people, a hard day, or emotional upset – will continue to happen in life. But the following chapters have you covered, so read on.

Summary

- Replacing old routines with new routines that support being alcohol-free makes life much easier.
- Complete your *TREAT Schedule*, to make sure your good intentions turn into actions.
- Don't wait until you can do everything perfectly. Just make a start and do your best. Concentrate on habits that help keep you alcohol-free. You can work on other healthy habits of your choice when you are feeling more secure in an alcohol-free lifestyle.

The Most Important Distance You Will Ever Travel.

I am not talking about the distance between cities, countries, or continents. I am talking about a much shorter distance. About 6 inches. This is the distance between your ears. What goes on here will change your life much more than moving hundreds or thousands of miles. If you travel from one part of the world to another, you take yourself with you. Your surroundings change, but you stay the same.

So far, I have discussed how to build new actions into your routine – how to change your behavior. This is a start. But new behaviors won't last if the underlying thinking is old thinking. Therefore, you need to change your *thinking* as well as your behavior. Otherwise, sooner or later, your old thinking will cause your new behavior to revert to being like old behavior.

The problem is that you cannot solve your problem with the same thinking that caused it.

However, if you change your *thinking,* everything will change. Your actions will change. Your attitudes will change. And these changes will have limitless knock-on effects.

It is not as simple as replacing old negative thinking with new positive thinking, although this will help. The first stage of changing your thinking is being *aware* of what your thoughts are now and how you respond to them. That's what we will do in this chapter.

In the early days of being free from alcohol, your thoughts will probably be all over the place. You might have intense cravings and feel stressed because you feel uncomfortable. You know you don't want to drink, yet you might still feel sorely tempted to drink. This is an uneasy place to be.

On top of that, you might still be dealing with the fallout from your last drinking episode, and it all feels like too much. Facing this nasty mix of internal turmoil and external trouble can seriously undermine your chances of staying sober.

With all these pressures, especially in the early days of sobriety, it is not surprising that you will have thoughts about drinking. Let me repeat that: You *will* have thoughts about a drink. But just because you have a thought or even an intense craving, does not mean you need to act on it.

So, in this chapter, I deal with the type of thinking that is most troublesome in early sobriety – thoughts about drinking. I call these types of thoughts *craving thoughts*, the type of tortuous thinking that centers on alcohol. These thoughts can take the form of random ideas that pop into your mind or endless mental gymnastics, rationalizing a drink. Your thinking can also be in direct response to triggers. Common triggers for cravings are sadness, boredom, certain people, and times and places where you usually drink. Your thinking can certainly undermine your efforts to remain alcohol-free and disturb your peace of mind.

The Most Important Distance You Will Ever Travel.

Craving thoughts in the early days of being alcohol-free are intense and intrusive because of the way our brains are wired. The reward center in your brain loves to get the booze. It lights up, buzzes, rings, and flashes. So, to make you keep supplying the addictive substance, the reward center sends you a craving thought. You have the thought, and you drink. You have taught your brain that this works. This reward center is like a toddler who demands sweets in the store. If he screams and cries and you supply the sweets, he learns that screaming and crying work. So, your brain learns that if it fires out a thought such as ''A glass of wine would be lovely'' and you drink the wine, that thought works. Your brain got the reward it craved.

So, it does it again.

And again.

Every time we drink, we make the connection stronger. When you *don't* drink your brain will be shouting like an unruly toddler," Where's my reward?" Craving thoughts will be stronger in the first few days because your brain has gotten used to sending out the thought and getting the reward. This is the cycle of addiction.

To make matters worse, when you are actively involved in routine drinking, you have physical symptoms to deal with too. At this stage, it's not just in your head. You get intoxicated, suffer physical withdrawal, and become obsessed about drinking again just to feel okay. And so it goes on....

The way to break the cycle is to ride out the period of withdrawal and weaken the hold alcohol has over your body and mind. Even if the thought of a drink feels intense, it *will* pass. And the longer you go without a drink, the less bothersome your cravings will be. It's like dealing with that demanding toddler. If you stand firm and don't give in, the child will learn you are no pushover, and the demands will become less frequent and less intense.

Craving thoughts will pop up from time to time, even for the person who has been sober for long period. So, it is useful to learn how to deal with these types of thoughts whether you are one-day sober or one-year sober. Post-Acute Withdrawal Syndrome (PAWS) is a medically recognized phenomenon. This means having occasional cravings for anything up to two years after the last drink is a normal part of this syndrome. Cravings are an expected aspect of life after heavy alcohol consumption, so there is no need to panic. Just don't give in to the cravings. If you do, you set off the cycle again. So, learning skills to deal with cravings is key to long-term success if you want to stay alcohol-free.

Craving thoughts can seem random and chaotic. What we do is apply some order to these seemingly disorderly thoughts, learning to observe them like a scientist observing an experiment. This takes out the emotional intensity. When you start to look at the thoughts more objectively, you will see that craving thoughts usually fall into one of 4 types:

1. The pesky itch thought: "I just can't stop myself from drinking." Or "I would feel less irritable if I had a drink." Or "I need a drink so much, I can almost taste it." These thoughts are like an itch. They keep coming up again and again. These can be

The Most Important Distance You Will Ever Travel.

the most annoying type of thought. It feels like you are being compelled to drink. These thoughts are **COMPULSIVE.**

2. The thoughts that pop into your mind when you see a chance to have a drink or obtain it for later. Thoughts such as "I could sneak off to buy a bottle later when I am walking the dog." Or "If I could buy a carton of wine while I'm doing the shopping, there would be no bottles to get rid of. No one would know." Or "I will be home on my own next Tuesday night. I could have a drink then." These could start as a random thought, but your old way of thinking sees an **OPPORTUNITY** to fit in a drink. If you latch on to the thought, it will grow and get stronger.

3. Then there are the thoughts that **PROMISE** how much better you will feel if you had a drink. But this is a false promise. These thoughts sound like, "If I had a drink, it would put me in a better mood." Or "I have a good time when I drink." Or "I can socialize more easily with a drink."

4. Lastly**, EMOTIONAL** thoughts: "I'd feel less anxious if I had a drink." Or "I need a drink to cheer me up." These thoughts use a bad mood or feeling low to get you to drink.

Use this information about types of thoughts to categorize them. Categorizing your thoughts in this way helps you stay a step ahead. This is because you will be using the rational part of your brain. By catching the thoughts early, you can respond to them more calmly before the greedy reward center of the brain takes over. You use your rational brain as a type of net to catch the thoughts before you act on them.

When a drinking thought pops into your mind, you can practice looking at it and working out what type of thought it is. This gives you time to pause before acting on the thought. These few seconds help the craving to lose its intensity. Your brain learns that you can have a thought of a drink and *not* drink. So next time you have the thought of a drink, your brain accepts that you might *not* have a drink and doesn't get so excited about the thought.

In addition, by using your brain to work out what type of thought it is, you end the struggle. You are not in a war with your thoughts. You are not using willpower. You sidestep the fight and just look at the thought like a puzzle piece you want to find a place for.

To help you memorize the four different types of thoughts I have a memory aid for you:

COPE.
This stands for:

C – **Compulsive** thoughts, the sort that feels like that annoying itch that won't go away.

O – **Opportunity** thoughts. You have the opportunity to drink.

P – **Promise** of feeling better or improving a situation. In reality, this is a false promise.

E – **Emotional** thought.

Brenda shared how she used 'COPE' to deal with craving thoughts. This is how she described her experience:

The Most Important Distance You Will Ever Travel.

"In the first few months of stopping drinking, I was constantly having thoughts of a drink. These thoughts bothered me, and I was worried about drinking again. I couldn't risk drinking again as I was on a warning at work. I had taken a lot of time off due to hangovers and even turned up to work drunk a couple of times.

Sometimes I was just in the supermarket and a thought would pop into my mind such as: 'I could get a box of wine and save it for Saturday. I'd be okay for work on Monday.' I would then take a moment to think, 'What sort of thought is that? Ah, it's an opportunity thought.' I would see it for what it was and by the time I did that, the thought would pass. In the old days, I would have played around with that thought and convinced myself it was okay to buy the wine. Nowadays, I remind myself that just because I could drink, doesn't mean I should drink. I could drink but I chose not to.

A weak point in my day would be the late afternoon when I arrive home from work. If I got home to an empty house and felt a bit sad, I might have a thought such as: "A drink would make me feel better." Instead of brooding on that thought and turning it over in my mind, I would take a moment to consider what sort of thought it was. I would realize I had thoughts of a drink because I felt a bit low and lonely. I would say to myself, 'That's an emotional thought,' and instead of drinking alcohol I would have a cup of tea and ring a friend.

This way of dealing with craving thoughts turned into a bit of a game. I had pictures of four boxes in my mind's eye, each box had a label: Compulsive Thoughts,

Opportunity Thoughts, Promise Thoughts, or Emotional Thoughts. In time, when I got quicker with the game, the boxes were simply labeled **C.0.P.E.**

After I had a thought, I would mentally pop the craving thought into one of the boxes. It helped me get rid of the thought. Looking at it in this way, the craving thought lost a lot of its power over me."

Another woman, Julia, used 'COPE' in a different way. She used it to help sort out what type of thought it was and do something about it:

"After a few weeks of looking at my cravings like different types of thoughts, I realized I was constantly having emotional thoughts. My cravings were usually about wanting to feel more comfortable, happier, or less stressed.

I discussed this realization with my recovery coach, and she suggested I spend some time putting together a list of ideas to help me deal with troublesome emotions and stress relief.

I started to do some yoga and breathing exercises and took a course in aromatherapy. These practices all helped me feel calmer and less stressed, and even if I was at work or out in public, I could take a few moments to do a breathing exercise to feel less stressed. Categorizing my thoughts helped me work out what I needed."

Much of the content in this book is aimed at continuing to change your thinking, so keep reading. In part two of the book, there is an additional chapter on dealing with

The Most Important Distance You Will Ever Travel.

cravings. In that chapter, there are a plethora of practical ideas to tackle thoughts that are urging you to drink.

Summary

- Your thinking is the driver of your behavior. To sustain the change, you need to change the thinking that has caused you problems.
- The first stage of changing thinking is to be aware of your thoughts and how you respond to them.
- You can become aware of the thoughts that cause the most trouble in early sobriety and use the COPE method to respond to them in a way that supports your efforts to remain alcohol-free.

From Fantasy Island to the Land of Your Dreams.

When it comes to past events, we often look back on our earlier life through a fantasy lens. This could be a rose-tinted one that makes the past look all cozy and sweet, and you might think, "Well, maybe my drinking wasn't that bad after all." Or it could be the opposite – we look back and only see all the bad stuff. This is a sort of selective memory that stirs up self-pity to rationalize drinking, leading to thoughts like, ''Poor me, poor me, pour me a drink."

Fantasy thinking about the future is usually vague and without substance. Someone might dream of being the type of person to run a marathon, but if they are drinking a bottle of vodka a day, running a marathon will not happen anytime soon. Someone else might engage in thoughts of giving up the booze tomorrow, next week, or next year. But that fantasy never happens, and they are doomed to have a lifelong alcohol problem.

As for fantasy thinking in the present, you might think something like, "I'm only going to have one drink today and leave it there." For some people – those annoying people often referred to as 'normal' drinkers – that might be realistic. But, if you are not one of those people and your drinking never stops at one drink, then it is fantasy thinking. You are deluding yourself and will likely end up drinking as much as usual.

True, we can use our daydreams and fantasies to create a reality we want, but it will never happen if dreaming is all we do. That's why this book is based on a plan. You need a plan to make your dream of being alcohol-free a reality. So don't let fantasy thinking derail you. You can use your imagination to envision the life you want, but you need to do the work to achieve it.

I once heard it said that imagination is like fire. If we use it with careful intention, it is extremely useful. But if we let it run rampant, with no focus or motive, it will be destructive and all-consuming. We can harness our imagination and fantasies for our benefit, but if we are blindly living our lives, mislead by our fantasy thinking, we will end up feeling bewildered and defeated.

We can utilize fantasy to fuel our dreams, enjoy downtime, cope with stress, and shape our future. But it needs to be done with awareness and intention. Without awareness, fantasy thinking will obscure issues we need to deal with, creating confusion and disappointment.

Elsewhere in the book, I urge you to make sure you have a support network. Get a sober coach, sponsor, counselor, or therapist to talk through your reflections on the past and your ambitions for the future. Use these people as a sounding board to test whether you are being realistic or indulging in fantasy thinking.

You might have clung to the idea that you could drink safely and happily. You might have said, ''I can stop anytime I want.'' You might have resisted the idea that your drinking was a problem. This type of fantasy thinking is called denial. You might know people who are in denial. It is frustrating and perplexing to see people destroy themselves and deny there is an issue.

The most common type of fantasy thinking with alcohol is, "This time it will be different." If the last time you drank there were arguments, work problems, accidents, or brushes with the law, why would it be any different this time or the next time you drink? Or you might still glamorize alcohol. When you imagine a big night out or a fancy occasion, perhaps it loses its sparkle for you if there is no booze involved.

Dalia, a woman I talked to about this book, spoke about her fantasy thinking with enthusiastic identification:

"Yes, that was me exactly! I always thought I had problems drinking because I was tired, or because someone made me angry. That's why I was argumentative. What messed up my thinking was that the bad things didn't happen every single time I drank – just most of the time! Sometimes I could have a couple of drinks and go home. But that took a lot of effort, and I would 'reward' myself the next time I drank with a big blowout, thinking I deserved to let my hair down. When I got into that reckless frame of mind, I always ran into problems. It was never different."

This type of fantasy thinking can persist, especially if you surround yourself with people who think the same way. The fantasy becomes normal.

Letting go of fantasy thinking is fundamentally about honesty – being honest about yourself, your drinking, what you want, and what you can reasonably expect of life and other people. Honesty isn't about being a goody-two-shoes. Being honest helps us to feel more comfortable about who we are.

Brain imagery has shown how being honest helps us to make better decisions and choices and keeps impulsivity in check – all good if we want to kick the booze. When we engage in endless fantasies and block out the reality of our situation, the pre-frontal cortex – which is the part of the brain responsible for skills such as thinking through options, coming to conclusions, and getting organized – gets damaged.

When alcohol is consumed addictively, the more primitive part of our brain (called the limbic brain) is running the show. That part of the brain is like a bad-tempered, greedy monkey. It demands to be fed instantly, is impulsive, and craves drama and excitement. This creates a self-defeating cycle. We crave alcohol and are dishonest with ourselves and other people. We are not dishonest because we are bad people. We dodge the truth so that we can rationalize drinking. The result is that all this fantasy and dishonesty weakens the very part of the brain that we use to make rational, beneficial choices.

However, if we confront fantasy thinking and get honest with ourselves, we break this cycle. So it's not all about being worthy and wholesome. Being honest is good for our brains and our well-being. Being honest with yourself means not pretending to be something you are not. This saves you a lot of emotional pain. For example, let's say you fantasize about being a marathon runner. But if you are simply not physically up to it, the mismatch between your fantasy and reality causes a sense of discontent and self-criticism. If you use alcohol to deal with the frustration of fantasy/reality mismatches in your life, you know where these uncomfortable sensations will lead – right back to the bottle.

You might have fantasies about what other people want from you, or who they expect you to be. For instance, let's say you fantasize that your boss thinks you are wonderful and is going to give you a promotion. Then you have an appraisal where she focuses on your faults, and painful reality kicks in. You might get angry with your boss, but the fault is not with her. It's your fantasy thinking that has caused the pain. This leads to discomfort and discontent – and more drinking.

To work out what sort of person you are and what you can realistically aspire to be, spend a few moments examining what you like and admire to help you get real. What do you hope to become? If you could be the best version of yourself, what would that look like? This is using your imagination to your advantage. You are creating an ambitious but realistic vision of yourself rather than a hopeless fantasy. Then carrying out a plan can turn your vision into reality. Reading and following the suggestions in this book will put that reality within your grasp.

Letting go of fantasy thinking also means we must make space for life to throw curve balls. It is a fantasy to think we can control other people or all factors in life. Understanding this is crucial for the problematic drinker as it's these factors that are out of our control that often upset us and act as a trigger to drink.

However, we do have some control. We can control our behavior, how we react to our thoughts and emotions, and how we show up in the world. We can also have some influence over some people in our lives. But we can't control them, and neither should we try.

Accepting these realities means we can maintain emotional balance if people behave in ways that upset, puzzle, or frustrate us. Accepting this means we don't get caught up in fantasies that hurt us because they are so mismatched with reality. Letting go of these types of fantasies makes us more resilient and less likely to drink. This is because we are not so disappointed by people or life in general, and we are more realistic about what we can expect from others.

To raise awareness of your fantasy thinking, spend a few minutes considering the following:

- What fantasies do you have about alcohol?
- Do you glamorize drinking?
- Do you tell yourself your drinking will be different this time, even though experience would indicate otherwise?
- Do you have fantasies about who or what you should be?
- Do you have unrealistic expectations about other people?
- Do you have unrealistic expectations about what life should give you?
- Do you see your past as all good or all bad? Or do you see it as a mixture of experiences,

opportunities, fond memories, and some challenges too?

- In what ways will you use the power of your imagination positively?
- If you have dreams or aspirations to improve your life, what can you do to make them a reality?

Vague fantasy thinking that is not in line with what you rationally want for yourself wastes precious time. It leads to activities that eat away our energy. Everything just seems too much effort when we are hung over. Opportunities slip through our fingers because we are too ill or drunk to grasp them. But you can harness the power of your imagination for positive outcomes.

Cravings for alcohol can be powerful and undermine your attempts to get or stay sober. Our imagination can help us to overcome these types of thoughts.

You can use your imagination to play out a story.

The story of: You Having a Drink.

Your craving mind will be eager to flash up pictures of you enjoying a drink. Fantasy thinking will kick in – big time. But let your mind carry on with the story of *You Having a Drink* right to the final scene of the story. The story could be you having dinner with your significant other in a restaurant. You get a craving to have wine with dinner. You could use your imagination to set the scene: the candlelight, the smiling face of your loved one, the ruby-red liquid in the crystal glasses, the sparkle of the silverware. It's all so perfect. A romantic scene of a couple sharing a meal and a bottle of top-quality red wine. You see it as sophisticated, classy, and grown-up.

But hang on!

Let's fast forward to the final scene of the story. How will it play out if you have the wine? Will it *just* be one or two glasses? Will the smile on your face stay soft and kind? Will you whisper sweet nothings to your loved one and float home on a cloud of happiness and delight? What will happen in reality? What has happened before in this type of situation? Use your imagination to recreate the sour turn the mood will take. The arguments, the scene out in the street, and the irrational anger that seems to come out of nowhere. Is that the story you want?

Now re-run the story. The first scene is the same – the candlelight, the table setting the smiles – but you have sparkling water in your glass. Let the scene play out with the sober you. There are no guarantees, but it would be more realistic to expect the evening to end happily if you are sober, so let your mind construct this happy picture of an enjoyable evening out.

Another way to use the power of fantasy constructively is to use imagery to relax. (Elsewhere in the book, I talk about methods to relieve stress. Guided imagery is a perfect way to do just that.)

Imagine you are in a beautiful place. It can be anywhere you like. Let your creativity run riot. Some people say they find visualization hard. If you find it difficult to use your visual imagination, use another sense that works for you. For example, you might hear the ocean and smell the tang of the sea air.

On the website of my publisher, WinsPress.com, there are various guided imagery meditation audios you can listen to for free. You can find them under the 'free stuff' tab on the website.

So, before you move on to the next chapter or close this book today, take a few moments to think about how you use your imagination. Is it fantasy thinking?

Used correctly, your imagination can take you from a fantasy island to the land of your dreams.

Summary

- Most of us engage in fantasy thinking at some time – about our lives, goals, others' opinions of us, and especially about our drinking.
- Fantasy thinking can be used intentionally and positively. It can help us to get motivated, relax and support an alcohol-free lifestyle.
- Over the next few days, be aware of when you daydream or fantasize How are you using the power of your imagination?

Swapping Out Your Beer Goggles.

"When I was drinking, I could not accept the idea that an alcohol-free life could be interesting or exciting. To me, even the word 'sober' sounded dull. In truth, I was frightened of not having the booze to fall back on as a crutch. I thought it lifted me when I felt down, helped me sleep, perked me up, and gave me the courage to talk to people.

I overlooked the fact that often when I drank, it was excessive, and I got angry and would start arguments. I just skimmed over these incidents and made excuses. I would tell myself I was only tired or stressed and that's why the bad things happened. Now that I am sober for over a year, I can hardly believe that was the way I thought. After a few days of stopping drinking, my head cleared, and I saw what I was doing to myself and my life. It was like putting on a pair of glasses that helped me see things clearly – or I should say, I took off my beer goggles!"

That is how Soria summed up her fundamental mindset shift. As she related the above to me, the earnestness of her expression conveyed the depth of her feeling. She shook her head in bewilderment as she reflected on how convinced she had been that life would be empty without booze. She continued:

"My dad ran the local pub in our village, and I grew up around heavy drinkers. My mother worked behind the bar. Often, at the end of the night, she and my dad would argue, but I just thought that was part of being a grown-up. I didn't question it. Both my parents were heavy smokers and lived on takeaways and fried breakfasts. I thought everyone lived this way. Seeing my dad down nine or ten beers during an evening was normal. When I moved away to go to college, my life continued in the same way. All my college friends were heavy drinkers, and I later married a drinker. I see now that I believed that a drinking lifestyle was how everyone lived. I couldn't imagine any other way of life."

Soria's experiences as a child and young person fueled her beliefs that excessive drinking was the norm. These beliefs had a powerful effect on her life. She was unaware of how they had directed her thinking and behavior for many years. Soria accepted arguments and poor health as part of life. In addition, she related how as a child she had looked after her parents while they were drunk or hungover. As an adult, she had done the same for her husband and had not questioned it. When Soria got sober, she looked at her life and her choices with fresh eyes. She realized how many of her choices were directed by what she believed about drinking and being female. This is the power beliefs hold over us.

As with Soria, the beliefs we hold about ourselves have a powerful effect on how we behave. This includes what we believe about other people and the world. The most powerful beliefs are usually the ones that are rooted deep in our subconscious. These beliefs can direct our thinking, choices, and reactions.

We have all absorbed many unhelpful beliefs about how we *should* show up in the world. This includes how we think we *should* behave, how we *should* look, and the roles we take on. On top of that, beliefs can fuel entrenched, unhealthy drinking behavior. Therefore, it is essential to identify and root out the beliefs that are sabotaging your efforts to stay alcohol-free.

To make matters worse, when we have deeply held beliefs, we look for evidence to justify them. For example, if you believe that you are boring without a drink, you will remember all the painful social experiences you had when you were sober. You will focus on the time you couldn't think of something to say to a person you had just met at a party, or you got tongue-tied. But you will forget about the times you chatted happily with friends when the only beverage on offer was coffee. Your mind is selective that way.

Do you see alcohol as having lots of advantages? Do you focus on how it changes how you feel? Do you think it makes you look glamorous or independent? Your mind turns a blind eye to the hangovers, arguments, financial costs, and work problems.

Beliefs about your character can be especially powerful. Your beliefs about yourself will affect how you present yourself, how you behave, and even how you let others treat you. So uncovering and changing unhelpful beliefs can transform your life.

Consider this: In India, the traditional technique to train a baby elephant to become compliant was to tie her to a post from an early age. The little elephant learned quickly that it was useless to tug at the rope that was tethering her to a strong post. After a period, the elephant stops pulling to get free and just accepts that she is unable to break free. When the elephant is older, the rope attaching the elephant to the post is untied. You would think she would bolt for freedom, but the elephant stays put. She remains by the post because she *believes* she cannot leave. The elephant has learned that every time she tugs to move away, she will be bound to the post. So, she gives up and stays by the post.

As people, we can be like that. We form beliefs in a certain time and situation and then, even when those circumstances have passed, we still hold on to the belief. The outdated belief remains, directing our thoughts and actions.

For instance, there might have been a time in your life when you used alcohol to support you through troubled times – such as a loss or relationship breakdown – and now you believe that you cannot live without it. But is that true? Or has alcohol trained you to believe that you cannot escape? In reality, like the elephant, you can simply walk away.

Joelle shared the following insight with me that will help demonstrate how powerful beliefs can affect our drinking behavior:

''For years I was completely baffled about my drinking. I just couldn't understand how I could be so disciplined in every other area of my life, and yet when it came to drinking, I seemed to just lose any sense of control. I have a college degree, various professional qualifications, and a job in HR for a high-profile company. I don't drink on weeknights as I need to be on the ball for work. I stick to an exercise plan and a healthy diet, yet when it comes to booze at the weekends, I just lose the plot. I am really worried as my drunken sprees are affecting my reputation at work and I recently drove while under the influence. Why is it that I can be so controlled in my work-a-day life, but once I uncork the bottle on a Friday night, all control flies out the window?''

Joelle talked through what happened in a typical week:

''Sundays I do a boozy brunch and sleep in the afternoon. Sunday evenings are hell. I feel anxious about the week ahead and groggy from the booze. I never sleep well on Sunday nights. I've lost count of the amount of Monday mornings I have decided to stop drinking. Sometimes I will think ahead and book up a fitness class or spa treatment for a Friday night, but I always cry off and go to the bar instead. On Friday afternoons at work, I am watching the clock, willing the hands to get round to 5 pm so I can break free and meet my drinking pals in the bar.''

As Joelle continued, it transpired that she had numerous attempts to control her drinking at weekends or stop it altogether. The efforts at control were not successful and she couldn't stop for more than a couple of weeks. But Joelle worked through a process of recovery. Part of this was dealing with entrenched beliefs. I will let Joelle explain how her beliefs were shaping her behavior.

''As I worked through a plan of recovery, I realized how much my early life had molded my behavior. My father died when I was ten. I had four younger siblings. My mother found it hard to cope with his death and her responsibilities. We struggled as a family, and I took on the role of mother at home. I cleaned, did odd jobs, looked after the little ones, and was super disciplined. I used to get up at 5 am to deliver newspapers before I went to school. I studied hard and didn't socialize as a teen.

When I moved away from home, I started to drink, but only at parties. I became a bit of a party girl and would let my hair down. I had two personas: The girl who was the clubber, the party animal, a bit wild. But Monday to Friday I was a diligent, serious, and very controlled professional. I even had different wardrobes for these identities. Often, people who saw me in both roles wouldn't recognize me between the two different images. Mostly, I had a distinct set of friends who drank like I did and would not raise an eyebrow at my extreme behavior. I had a separate set of friends related to work. Rarely did these worlds collide, but when they did, people were often confused and shocked.

Once I stopped drinking and did some work on my beliefs, I realized that one of my core beliefs was that I had to be in control and that the only way I could let go was to get drunk. Since having this insight, I have been able to find ways to relax and enjoy myself without drinking, and I have eased up a bit on the control issues I have at work and in my relationships.

This realization has not only helped me to overcome drinking, but it has also made my life much more enjoyable and my relationships much more relaxed. I am embarrassed to admit how much of a control freak I was, and I had no idea how I was coming across and how this impacted my behavior around alcohol.''

Joelle had mixed beliefs about herself, some that seemed to contradict others, adding to her feelings of confusion. For example, she thought of herself as both a party girl and a serious, professional woman. She had an entrenched belief that the only way she could relax and let go was to get drunk. Her beliefs about herself were directing her thoughts and her behaviors. The results were feelings of inauthenticity, embarrassment, and confusion. She also had an overwhelming compulsion to hit the bar on a Friday night. Often, she would be out of pocket when she canceled classes or spa sessions at the last minute. Her rational mind was not controlling her behavior, but her beliefs *were*.

So how do you change beliefs?

The first step in changing beliefs is awareness. It is tricky to be aware of beliefs that have become so ingrained we don't even see them anymore. To make it easy, you look at what you can see and hear. Spot the type of thoughts you have and listen to what comes out of your mouth. You need to look at your thoughts and be aware of the words you use about yourself. So, awareness of your beliefs means you need to look at your thoughts, words, and the labels you apply to yourself. Watch your self-talk.

Now, let's unpick what all that means in practice. How do you watch your thoughts, words, and self-talk?

It might feel like watching your thoughts is like performing mental gymnastics and it makes your head hurt. But don't *try* to watch them. Just relax and get on with your day. As you go about doing your usual stuff, simply notice the thoughts that come into your mind.

Doing this will uncover your beliefs. And this habit of looking at your thoughts will also help you have more mastery over random ideas that pop into your mind – thoughts such as, ''A drink would be a great idea''.

Many of us slip into the habit of having a thought and getting completely wrapped up in it. When this happens repeatedly, it is hard to distinguish between ourselves as individuals and the mental chatter. We end up being pushed around by our thoughts. They take over. Life can feel chaotic. We feel we are at the mercy of random cravings. The thoughts can feel like they are *who* we are. But they are not. They are just thoughts.

Let's go back to Joelle to demonstrate how to apply these ideas. Since childhood, Joelle had millions of thoughts along the lines of: "I am responsible for my family. I can't relax. I must be ultra-disciplined to get everything done". She then became over-identified with the thought. The thoughts became *who* she was. The only way she could escape from its self-imposed bondage was to get drunk. By keeping the drinking to weekends only, she felt she was applying some control, but this was an illusion.

To help you to uncover your beliefs, you need to distinguish between your thoughts and *yourself. You* as the real, authentic self, and *you* under all the layers of labels and beliefs. The beliefs that drive your behavior.

If this is difficult to grasp, let's use the analogy of eating a cookie. You are not the cookie, just as you are not the thought. You look at the cookie, and you observe it. You can smell and taste the cookie. You can experience it. If you eat the cookie it will pass through your digestive tract, but you will never 'be' the cookie. Likewise, your thoughts will pass through your mind, but you are not your thoughts – they are meant to come and go. Just as you look at the cookie, you can look at your thoughts. You can experience the thought by being aware of the effect it has on you. By watching your thoughts, you can start to spot patterns that give you clues as to the beliefs that you have built up and might be unaware of.

Earlier in the book, I talked about triggers. You will remember I introduced COPE to catch those triggering thoughts without acting on them. No doubt you will have had the experience of a trigger thought popping into your mind, randomly. 'Where did that come from?!' you might ask. Those random drinking thoughts are most likely rooted in a belief you hold deep in your subconscious. For example, let's look at the experience of Sheryl:

Sheryl had stopped drinking for a couple of months. She was happier not drinking and felt that her mood, health, relationships, and work-life had all improved. However, she was shocked when she had a sudden strong urge to drink when she landed in another city for a work meeting. She had to stay overnight, which she had done before and wasn't concerned about. She just watched the thoughts and let them go. Later that night she phoned me and talked it through.

She was worried about being unable to talk confidently with her clients. She realized she believed deep down that she was inarticulate and boring. She had been a shy, awkward teenager with a stammer and this fear had never really left her. Together, we challenged these beliefs and I reminded her of how well she could communicate ideas, which was true.

If you do have unhelpful thoughts, question them. Ask if they are true. Consider what they mean. Do they lead to self-pity, self-recrimination, or an "I'm not worth recovery" type feeling that leads you right back to a drink?

Watch your self-talk. Do you put yourself down or over-apologize? Be aware of self-sabotage. Do you set yourself up to make a belief true? This is an example of self-sabotage. Are you constantly running late, losing things, or being generally disorganized? This may be because you have taken on the belief that you are scatty and your life is all over the place. "Hey, no wonder I drink!" you might quip. "I can't even make it to work on time!"

Over the next few days, notice the names you call yourself. When you have a few, say five or six, check them. Are they helpful? Do they give you excuses to drink or act out? For example, Sheryl realized she had a habit of calling herself a 'dumb blonde' as a joke.

Listen to how you talk to other people. Do you find yourself trying to say what you think someone wants to hear? Do you find yourself agreeing when you want to disagree? Or stating an opinion that you don't believe? Or going along with other people to avoid rocking the boat? Ask yourself why you are not holding to your own opinion or beliefs and try to uncover why you don't feel safe enough to share who you are.

When you have spent a few days watching your thoughts, self-talk, and conversations with other people, take some time to work through the following exercise. This exercise is about nailing down the beliefs you want to change. More importantly, it is about changing them.

This would be an ideal exercise to do during the reflection part of your daily actions.

Changing Beliefs

First, take a piece of paper and write these headings: 'Me,' 'Alcohol,' and 'Other People.' Next, write down the first three ideas or sentences that come to mind. Don't over-analyze. I mean literally, the first words that pop into your mind. These are the beliefs you hold.

Now pick one sentence or phrase from each heading. You will now have three beliefs you have identified. If you want to change them, think about what action you could take to overturn the belief.

Soria, who we met earlier, kindly shared some of the results she had doing this exercise. She watched how she talked to herself and other people. She became more aware of her habitual actions. This is what she came up with:

Me:

I don't feel like I am worth the trouble of getting sober.

Action: Follow 'The Plan' every day and treat myself well.

Alcohol:

I need it to function.

Action: Deal with cravings. Avoid drinking and prove to myself that I can function without alcohol.

Other People:

Other people will only love me if I put up with their bad drinking behavior.

Action: Stop making it easy for my husband to drink to excess. Let him deal with the consequences of his behavior.

For example, Soria believed that other people only loved her if she put up with them drinking excessively. Soria had taken care of her parents when they were hungover. As an adult, she never complained no matter how much her husband drank or how hungover he was. She even rang work for him when he was sick from drinking. She stopped doing this. The next time her husband asked her to ring work with excuses, she refused. If he got too drunk to get to bed, Soria stopped taking off his shoes and getting a blanket for him when he was passed out on the sofa.

Soria realized that she could function better without alcohol. She got to know other sober people and saw that not everyone drinks. She learned to treat herself with care and respect by doing caring things for herself, and she learned that she was indeed worth making the effort to get sober. She did this by working on being aware of her beliefs and with action. She changed her behavior. In turn, it was easier to change her behavior because she was working on changing her beliefs. Soria repeats this exercise from time to time as part of her reflection and finds the results helpful as she continues to enjoy her alcohol-free life.

Changing your beliefs can take time. But every time you challenge an unhelpful belief, you weaken alcohol's hold on you. Until you are no longer like the elephant who stays by the post despite being untethered. You can simply walk away.

Summary

- Repeated thoughts about ourselves become entrenched beliefs. These beliefs have a powerful effect on our behavior.
- To change beliefs, we need to be aware of them by looking at our thoughts, self-talk, and reflecting on our attitudes.
- Complete the written exercise (Me, Alcohol, Other People) to help uncover your beliefs. Act on changing them by changing how you respond to these beliefs.

Peeps, Pals, and Playmates.

Y ou are choosing to be alcohol-free to have a better life, not a lonely one. We all want to feel like we belong. From cave dweller campfires to online Facebook groups, people have always needed to connect with others. Being sober is an open door to fully enjoying life, and that includes having a social circle and events you look forward to.

We all want to have fun. We want pals and playmates. No one wants to be Ms. Noddy-No-Mates. This desire to enjoy life with friends is natural and there is no reason to be glum, anti-social, or a hermit just because you don't drink. I have lived in a few different countries and moved towns many times. I have made a string of friends along the way. I have never centered these friendships on drinking. I enjoy having female friends to meet for a coffee, have a chat, and share the good times and the bad times. Earlier in life, I was shy and self-conscious and had to learn how to make friends and be sober.

Most teenagers usually drink to fit in. I was a bit late to the party with this one. I was a quiet studious academic, and I held off drinking until my nineteenth birthday. My newfound university pals decided they would show me how to celebrate. This boozy event was a gateway for me. This was when I discovered the bonhomie and bonding that happens when a gang of friends gets loaded together.

At nineteen, we can pass off drunken antics and raucous behavior as teenage high spirits. Later in life, however, these escapades get harder to justify. The morning after the night before is harder to laugh off when you have a young family to attend to. The first day back to work after the one-woman-show at the Christmas office party is embarrassing when you are a working professional

You've probably experienced finding a new 'best friend' while drunk. You feel connected. It's fun. Where has this person been all your life? Everything they say cracks you up or sets off some sort of soulful recognition in you. You understand each other. You bond like glue.

But then you sober up. Snatches of the conversation flashback through your fractured memory the next day. You recall saying stuff you'd rather not have said. You look at your best buddy's selfies from the night before and cringe. Two drunk women with shiny faces, Alice Cooper makeup, and red noses with eyes to match. Next time you see your 'friend' in the grocery store, you dive down behind the shelves. Not much true bonding there.

Making friends without the crutch of alcohol worries many people new to sobriety. But, even if you feel that you are a raging extrovert and that making friends doesn't worry you, read this chapter. It will give you a fuller picture of how your social life will expand not contract when you go alcohol-free. You might be the sort of person who thrives in groups, but if your social life has become focused only on events that involve alcohol, you might be scratching your head thinking, ' *How do people have fun without booze?*'. Some people who would consider themselves an extrovert whilst pursuing a drinking career find out they are in fact the opposite as they settle into an alcohol-free life. They discover a richer inner life and don't feel the compulsion to be out with other people all of the time. They discover more balance in their life and enjoy quiet time alone. But whether you are a full-on extrovert, an introvert or somewhere in between, this chapter will give you some ideas on activities to enjoy that don't revolve around alcohol. There will also be some tips on how to enjoy events where alcohol is present, without feeling the need to indulge. So, keep reading.

However, that being said, social anxiety is real for many people, even those who seem confident on the outside. I know. I can remember meeting a group of new work colleagues in a bar in my early twenties. My legs were shaking so much under the table that the drinks were sloshing all over the surface. I'd have a sense of inner panic about what to say, how to appear, and I would stress out about people not liking me. The drink took that away. I understand how social anxiety feels.

The problem with using alcohol, especially in copious amounts, is that it can make us feel *too* free and easy. The tongue gets loosened up *too* much and we do and say things we later regret. The connection and bonding we crave are blown apart by *over*-sharing, *over*-friendliness, and *over*-the-top behavior. Most sane people back off.

If you become angry or aggressive whilst drunk, it's worse. You scramble together fragments of your furious outbursts from the night before, trying to work out how much to grovel in apology.

However, despite the drawbacks, many of us use alcohol to numb feelings of social anxiety. The problem is that as well as numbing the anxiety it is also numbing our ability to ensure our behavior stays within the range of what is proper. But even if we have embarrassed ourselves once due to drinking too much, we do it again and again. There must be a better way to manage social anxiety, overcome loneliness, and achieve the sense of belonging we crave. There is a better way. Millions of people have discovered that making friends, enjoying social occasions, and feeling a deep sense of connection and belonging are all possible in an alcohol-free life.

I didn't call it social anxiety back when I was in my twenties. I thought of it as a lack of self-confidence. I felt nervous about meeting new people in social situations. I was fine at work or in circumstances in which everyone had a defined role with set things to say. But put me in a group for fun and I clammed up. Age has helped me. I no longer have any problem talking to people – ask my husband! But looking back at my younger years, this type of anxiety played a big role in my desire to drink. Having a drink obliterated those uncomfortable feelings. The problem was it obliterated my social filters too. Filters that send out messages such as *"You've said enough"*, *"This person is not safe to talk to"* or *"Another drink is not a good idea."*

So, the following is some advice on overcoming social discomfort from someone who has been there and suffered from a racing heart, blushes, dry mouth, and shaky legs. Even if you are someone who does not struggle with any sense of social discomfort, the following tips will help you to enjoy events without alcohol. You can try some of these tips to help you feel more in the mood for a social gathering, without having to rely on alcohol to pep you up or calm you down:

As you prepare to go out to a social event or gathering, be upbeat. Play some bouncy music and decide to enjoy yourself. Pull out an outfit you like and above all feel comfortable in. Check if there are any dress codes to be aware of, but as most situations are casual these days, dress for comfort and in colors and styles you feel good in. Don't aim to impress. Just be tidy, clean, and comfortable so you can forget about how you look and relax as much as possible. Unless it is a formal affair, it is usually better to dress down a bit if you feel self-conscious. And I said dress down *a bit*. You don't need to slouch around like Ms. Frump.

The main thing is that however you express your style, you feel comfortable and confident. Ask yourself whether you are wearing the outfit, or is the outfit wearing you? If you feel self-conscious or even slightly discomfited by your clothes choice, change it into something you feel you can wear and forget about as you socialize.

Remind yourself that everyone else has their flaws, hang-ups, and worries. Remind yourself of this often. You might look at someone and think they appear confident and comfortable, but I bet if you got to know them well, they might admit to feeling quite different from how they appear. Usually, people are trying to present themselves in a good light, so bear that in mind. It is not usually how it seems.

When you are at a gathering and find yourself face to face with someone you don't know, make them feel important.

If you do that, you will accomplish two things: Firstly, you will take the pressure off yourself because the attention will be on the other person. Secondly, you will be a big social hit because people love to feel important.

How do you make someone feel important? You make them feel important by listening to their every word as if they are genius and you don't want to miss one little nugget of wisdom. Memorize their name and ask questions. Be interested, even if initially they don't seem your type or have a hobby or a job that doesn't interest you. You never know, as you get talking to them, they might turn out to do or know something that grabs you. So, keep an open mind. As you listen to the person, look at them. Have you ever talked to someone and their eyes keep darting about the room away from you as you are speaking? How did you feel? Now, think of someone who listens to you attentively. How does that make you feel? Be that person.

Lastly, if pesky thoughts come into your mind – such as: "They think I'm boring" or "They don't like me" – focus on what you see and hear in your surroundings. Ignore these thoughts. You are showing up as your best sober self. Don't let that nasty, spiteful inner critic voice get to you.

The next hurdle people talk about in early sobriety in the context of social life is loneliness. If all your pals are drinkers and your social life has revolved around your local drinking dens, you are going to need to adjust. Even if you think of yourself as a confident extrovert, building an alcohol-free social life *will be* an adjustment. But you don't need to feel lonely.

Loneliness is not limited to the newly sober. It is a modern epidemic. It is also a very subjective experience. Some people might enjoy time alone and see it as precious solitude. Others will endure a period on their own with a sense of isolation. If you are an introvert, you will feel energized by time spent on your own, doing individual activities. Your inner life is rich and fulfilling and loneliness is less of a problem. Extroverts, however, need to be with people to feel uplifted and rejuvenated. They feel loneliness more acutely. Ideally, a balance between alone time and time with others is healthy. So even if you enjoy time alone, push yourself a little out of your comfort zone to be sociable.

In addition to the amount of time with others, it is useful to consider the *type* of connections you make and aim for balance. I'm not talking about specific types of friendships but am referring to three broad categories of connection. These are: 1. Close, intimate connections with romantic partners or close friends. 2. More casual friendships 3. Collective connections such as with people at church or in your local community. Aim for a balance across the three.

For example, recently I lived abroad in a holiday location with my husband for six months. We do most things together and I enjoy that, so I wasn't exactly lonely – but I missed my female friends and doing things like going out with my running club, or attending local events, meet-ups, and meetings. I was looking forward to getting back to the town where we have our permanent home in the UK because I missed my girlfriends and being part of a community. So, if you just have a vague sense of loneliness, ask yourself whether it is an ache for an intimate partner, for friendships, or for feeling part of a wider group or community. Knowing which it is can help you take the right action.

There are so many ways to meet people nowadays, so put yourself out there. If you yearn for a deep connection with a soulmate, then getting out to events, classes, or doing sports that interest you means you are more likely to meet someone interested in the same things.

It takes time to get to know people. So, keep turning up, even if you consider the people, you meet are not as welcoming as you think they should have been. You might *think* they don't like you. It doesn't matter. Psychologists have worked out that in a group of seven people, two won't like you. That means out of seven people, two won't like me or like my next-door neighbor or my friend or whoever. So, stop fretting about people not liking you – it's just statistics.

That being said, there are many stages in a woman's life when making friends can be tricky. Being at home with a new baby or young children can feel isolating. If you are trying to get sober, the pressure of the 'mommy wine' culture can add to the sense of isolation and of not being part of the crowd. It can be hard to navigate. However, people might not be as interested in what is in your glass as you think they will be. Time and time again, I have found that the people who either try to push drink onto me or ask why I don't want an alcoholic drink, repeatedly, are usually the ones who are worried about their own drinking. The chapter in this book called *Draw Your Line in the Sand* has tips on managing this type of situation.

If you are at home with children, other mums will be too. Reach out and find out about toddler groups or new mum meetups. Having these sorts of contacts and friends is a lifesaver as a new mum, aside from getting sober. As well as online, check out information boards at your local doctor's office, churches, and community centers.

Nowadays, being alcohol-free is increasingly seen as a healthy lifestyle choice. So-called 'dry bars' are popping up in many towns and cities, so if you plan to meet a new friend, finding a venue like this can make it easier.

Many of the women I interviewed for this book described how joining women's running groups helped them. I am a member of women's running groups in the town where I live. I found them on Facebook I have made many lovely friends this way. Usually, there are beginners' groups who walk and run a little, so do go along, even if you struggle to run for the bus.

Your thing might be crafting or attending talks on subjects of interest. You might want to go back to church or try a meditation group. Whatever you decide to do, keep showing up. Attend meetings or events consistently. Take on a role such as making the tea or clearing up. That way, if before you go that little voice in your head tells you that you are too tired or too busy to attend, you will have committed to doing a task, so you will be more inclined to make the effort to go along.

When you give it some time and turn up consistently. When you listen to others and are interested in them, the magic will start to happen. You will find that sooner or later other people will respond to your honesty, openness, and positivity. They will listen to you. You will develop the rapport you have craved, and you will make friends – sober.

These friendships will be deeper, more caring, and more satisfying because they are about two people who are in control of what they say, remember what they have said and done, and are (most likely, but there are no guarantees) rational. When you meet them again you will be able to recall what you said and did, minus the embarrassment. These sorts of friends meet that need for connection we all have – a need to be seen, listened to, and understood.

In early sobriety, you might feel raw and socially awkward. That's okay. You are re-learning how to have a good relationship with people without booze. It takes time. Attending sobriety-centered meetings can help because you are all in the same boat and other people in the group will understand how you feel – even if you stammer, stutter, or turn bright red as you attempt to speak. They will understand the tumult of emotions you are feeling. You don't have to say anything, just listen and see how you feel about it. If you have tried AA and it is not for you, other meetings exist, such as SMART. Do a bit of googling for your local area and try some groups. It is worth a shot if you are struggling alone.

When we experience the first flush of sobriety – the clear head, the return of feelings such as excitement, joy, elation, and pleasure without a drink – it can feel giddy. If you find yourself rushing around to meetings, having coffee with your new best friends, and talking for hours on the phone, it can be intoxicating. It's like being a teenager again. But a wee word of caution here: Use your discretion. Trust your gut. Don't rush at it. You do not have to tell everyone you meet your full, unedited life story as soon as you meet them. Open up, but do it gradually.

Take your time to get to know people, especially other people in early recovery. Most will be beautiful souls who are glad to be on the same path as you, but some people might not be as well or as nice as you. There is an expression in recovery groups: *"Some people are sicker than others."* So, take it easy and if you get a bad vibe about someone, ease back. You are not obliged to go for coffee or meet up with anyone outside of a meeting if you don't want to. So just say no if that's what feels right for you. No apologies. This is especially relevant if a man keeps pestering you. It's creepy and not on. Blank them if you need to. If they don't get the message, have a word with another member of the group. You have a right to feel safe.

No doubt you will use online groups too, to get support and encouragement. These are brilliant tools but do make sure you establish some real-life friendships. It is easy to lurk around online groups. The problem with online activity is that it's easy just to delete your profile, leave a group or close an account and disappear. If someone is asking you to pay a subscription to join a group or offers some sort of online counseling, check out their credentials and ensure they have some sort of relevant professional background.

With all the alcohol-free choices and opportunities, we have for connection these days, there is no need to feel alone.

Summary

- Loneliness can be a major issue for newly sober people, as it can for many people.
- Work out how much time you need alone or with others and find a balance that works for you.
- Make it a priority to make connections (intimate, friendships, and community). Forge bonds with others in a way that fits in with your circumstances.

Stop Beating Yourself Up.

D o you feel you have to be ruthlessly self-critical to motivate yourself?

If that is the case, I have one question to ask you:

How is that working for you?

Seriously, has calling yourself rude names, beating yourself up for past mistakes, and giving yourself zero slack made you happy?

And – crucially – has it helped you get sober and stay sober? Or has it just given you excuses to drink more?

Many people feel they must push hard to get results. Pushing beyond endurance. That if we go to enough meetings, work a step (*again!*), do more service, get up at 4 am and run 10 miles, whatever, we will get well. These activities may well work, but if you are constantly criticizing yourself, the chances of sustainable success are low.

Thinking we can get well via the 'no pain, no gain' route is understandable. We try it that way because it feels like we are in control if we are putting in the effort. If we just *try* hard enough, if we put the work in, we will get well. We might do it, but if we hate ourselves in the process, it won't work in the long term. This sort of attitude is based on fear of what will happen if we fail. Thinking we can recover by being overly self-critical is based on an illusion of control. But self-criticism leads to a loss of faith in ourselves because we can't keep up the enormous efforts every day.

The antidote to this harsh self-criticism is self-compassion. It goes against the grain in our society to do what we can comfortably achieve and let go a little. But doing the work in recovery with an attitude of self-compassion builds self-confidence, which creates a safe space in which to examine our flaws and shortcomings. If we spot a character trait we would like to adjust, we see it in perspective. We accept we are a work in progress.

Self-compassion wants you to be healthy and happy. It is not an excuse to behave in ways that will hurt you. That includes acting out or drinking in a way that is harming your health or well-being. By being gentle and caring with yourself, you will make choices that enhance your wellbeing, so *self-compassion is foundational for recovery from alcohol issues*.

Many people confuse self-pity with self-compassion. Self-pity is a natural reaction to being at the sticky end of difficult events or circumstances. It's okay to feel sad or upset. Self-compassion will acknowledge this and provide the encouraging safe place you need to move on. Self-pity keeps you stuck in a 'poor me' funk. Nothing changes.

Self-compassion helps you feel comfortable and confident in getting up again and doing what you need to do to get past the difficult time. It gives you courage and strength. Self-pity tells you that you are a victim, and it portrays events in a way that is out of whack with reality.

You stay stuck in fear and sadness. Self-compassion helps you move on.

Although self-compassion might seem passive and fluffy, it is an attitude that provides momentum for action. It is also a skill that needs to be learned. Some years ago, I worked as a social worker with young people in care who had profound emotional and behavioral difficulties. Many of them had grown up in abusive families and were in care for their protection. These youngsters were accustomed to being criticized and treated harshly. Many were hyper-vigilant, distrustful, and anxious. They had never been taught how to self-soothe or relax. Some engaged in self-harming behaviors such as cutting and scratching themselves.

I share this because, even though these are extreme examples, they mirror in an exaggerated way what many people do when misusing alcohol. Drinking so much that we get sick, or doing things that cause us legal, financial, or social problems is a type of self-harm. We have learned to take a bashing.

You might well have accepted a crushing hangover or the consequences of a bender without considering the impact it was having on your health. If you work and have a family or caring responsibilities, you have probably learned to push through the sickness and headaches until you could get a drink again.

Your concept of self-care might have been a large gin and tonic or a bottle of wine – or two. If we have got caught in this trap, skills such as self-compassion and self-care need to be learned and practiced. Similarly, I had to teach the young people I worked with that it was safe to relax and that they could do things for themselves to be soothed and cared for. Slowly these youngsters learned that instead of harming themselves to find relief, they could run a warm bath, close the bedroom curtains, put on some calming music and fairy lights, or lie under a cozy blanket and listen to a story on an app – simple activities, but they needed to be taught.

You might have gotten so used to working hard, pushing through physical or mental discomfort, and using alcohol to comfort and reassure yourself that you have forgotten about simple things you can do to show yourself some necessary love.

Showing yourself some kindness is made up of self-soothing things you do. So, pause now and take a moment to reflect on the sorts of things you could do to show yourself some care. Now that you have stopped drinking, a plethora of activities is available to you. These activities do not have to be expensive or time-consuming. It is the *attitude* of self-compassion with which you carry them out that makes the difference. Even just taking a few minutes to allow yourself to enjoy a cup of coffee or tea, instead of rushing around and gulping it down, is an act of self-compassion.

A sober life is more enjoyable, not harder. Build in activities you find pleasurable and soothe stress. For many people, stress is a big trigger to drink, so look at these activities as ways to safeguard your sobriety, even if you feel self-indulgent.

As well as building in time for self-soothing activities in daily life, you can show yourself compassion by how you react to difficult feelings. This could be anything – perhaps you have taken a drink again and feel bad about it, or shouted angrily at your spouse or child and are beating yourself up for being mean. The following is a process to work through when these types of feelings come up:

First, just notice that you feel bad. Name how you feel: angry, disappointed, stressed, or full of regret, whatever it is. Register where and how you feel it in your body, such as a fast heart rate, a churning stomach, grinding teeth, or a headache. Take a moment to feel it.

Second, remind yourself that all human beings feel just like you do at some stage in their lives. You are not alone. Everyone gets upset, angry, disappointed, or stressed sometimes. It's normal.

Third, use supportive self-talk. Talk to yourself like you would talk to a friend or a loved one. Use words you would normally use to comfort someone if they were upset, such as "It will be okay." Or "It will get easier. You are doing good." Or "You tried your best. It will be better next time."

A gentle, more forgiving attitude towards yourself means you will have the courage to move forward and try again. You won't feel so defeated or unworthy. You will learn from the experience and use it as information to make things better in the future. Self-criticism will keep you stuck and afraid, so don't let it creep back in.

This process acknowledges our common humanity. This makes us feel less alone and isolated. This is an important point. It is important because perceiving ourselves as the only one who has ever felt a certain way is a lonely experience. Feeling odd, abnormal, or different from others, is a scary place to be. As humans, we want to feel part of the tribe to feel safe and connected. Therefore, acknowledging our feelings as a normal part of being human, helps us to feel less isolated.

To begin with, it will feel a bit strange to be more self-compassionate. But like any skill that is learned, it gets less clunky with practice.

If you feel you would like to learn more about self-compassion, you may be interested in my other books: *Mindfulness for Stress and Anxiety* and *Mindfulness for Alcohol Recovery.* These books have exercises and guided meditations to support you in building an attitude of self-compassion as a life skill to help you stay alcohol-free.

Summary:
- Relentless self-criticism undermines sobriety.
- Drinking excessive amounts of alcohol is an act of self-harm. It is essential to find alternative ways to deal with stress and disturbing feelings, which everyone experiences from time to time.
- Self-compassion and self-care are skills that can be learned and will help you stay sober and enjoy life.

Getting Your Feelings Back.

"The best thing about getting sober is getting your feelings back. The worst thing about getting sober is getting your feelings back." – Anon.

A drink can seem to pep us up if we're tired, give us a lift if we feel low, or take the edge off if we feel sad. Of course, the downside is that this apparent change in mood is short-lived, unpredictable, and usually ends up making us feel worse. But if we are used to drinking to deal with a bad mood, what should we do when alcohol isn't an option anymore?

Newly sober people often report feeling marvelous and life is good. But early sobriety can also have a tough side because, for the first time in years, we might feel emotions we had drunk to escape. Consequently, having a drink might become tempting, which can lead people right back to a drink. So, learning new ways to deal with challenging feelings is a key tool in staying sober.

Talking through your feelings and getting support is hugely encouraging. So, take a few moments to think about who you can talk to. Consider the intensity of your feelings and the duration of time you have felt any powerfully negative emotions. If it's been more than a few weeks and you feel low, reach out to a health professional. And if you have thoughts of self-harm or suicide, reach out today – now.

We are biological beings. Sorry if that makes us sound like washing powder, but it is true. We are made up of bodily systems that need daily maintenance in the form of decent food, hydration, sleep, rest, and movement. It's not rocket science. You probably don't need to cast your mind back too far to think of a time when you felt lousy, and the reason was you had a poor night's sleep, or you realized you had been bombing about fueled only on caffeine and fresh air. A few days of proper nutrition and you got your mojo back. But I mention it first here because even though it seems obvious, it is amazing how we can forget these basic facts.

Many people react to feelings of low mood, lack of energy, or mild depression with a Freudian approach. They conclude something deep and psychological must be going on when all they need to attend to is their physical health first. In part two of this book we will delve a bit deeper but for now, let's deal with the issues that are in plain sight, such as nutrition, exercise, sleep, rest, and hydration.

Don't worry – I am not going to tell you what to eat or how much water to drink or advise on the most efficient workout. There are plenty of books, videos, blogs, and internet sites giving all that sort of information. But this section is a gentle reminder to attend to the foundations first.

If you have fallen into the habit of not eating properly while drinking copious amounts of alcohol, your body will have taken a bashing. You might not even be consciously aware you are doing it. Commit to nurturing your body with nourishing food, healthy drinks, and rest.

In the early days of sobriety, don't get too wound up about the nuances of good health. Keep it simple. When I feel overwhelmed by the deluge of advice out there about health and feel the need to get back on track, I get back to basics. I follow, what I call *The Rule of 8* for a few days.

This means I drink 8 glasses of water, sleep for 8 hours a night, meditate or sit quietly for 8 minutes, walk 8 thousand steps a day, and eat 8 portions of fruits and vegetables every day. After a few days of this regime, my energy is usually restored, and my mood improves. (Of course, if you have specific health concerns you should follow the advice of your doctor.)

When you stop drinking, you might have nutritional deficiencies that are affecting how you feel, so getting some blood samples taken at the doctor can help uncover issues that might be bringing down your mood. Our emotions and moods can be strong indicators of what is going on physically, so attend to the physical aspects of your well-being as a preliminary response.

I see emotions as a sort of barometer. A barometer is a device that indicates what the weather is like. It tells us whether it is fine or stormy. Our emotions are barometers of our inner and outer life. For example, you might be feeling cranky due to a poor night's sleep or have a sense of sadness and loss because your dog had just died. When we experience these sorts of events and reactions, we can see cause and effect quite clearly. Many women struggle with intense feelings of irritability, low mood, anxiety and worry during the time of the month approaching menstruation and during the time of life around menopause. Recognizing that these powerful emotions are a reaction to hormonal fluctuations can help. There is no need to start psychoanalyzing. But a conversation with your doctor would be advisable. It's amazing the difference medication or supplements to address hormonal imbalances can make. So if you are feeling out of whack, it might be worth having a chat with your health care provider to address any hormonal issues.

Did you know that heavy alcohol consumption can increase levels of estrogen in the body? So when you stop drinking, estrogen levels can drop. Women who are going through perimenopause and menopause are especially sensitive to this as estrogen levels are lower to begin with. Carrying on drinking alcohol to avoid this drop in estrogen is a no-no as heavy alcohol consumption heightens the risk of breast cancer. So more reasons to avoid alcohol. However, the drop in estrogen when you stop drinking copious amounts of alcohol can affect your mood and outlook dramatically. Estrogen can affect brain chemicals such as serotonin, so there are clear links between how you feel emotionally and what is going on hormonally. So getting some blood work done to monitor the levels of hormones might help illuminate what is going on for you.

Regardless of the cause of a bad mood, it can be tempting to try to ignore or change the feeling simply because it's uncomfortable. When we have had years or decades of using alcohol to change a feeling or numb it, reaching for a drink becomes our default reaction. It will take time to establish new, healthier default responses. Getting a medical check-up and looking at ways to improve your nutrition, movement, sleep, and connections with others are all positive new habits to embed into daily life.

You have probably heard the expression *'This too shall pass.'* The problem with that saying is that when someone counsels you wisely with these very words, usually at a time when you feel most low, your initial reaction might be to punch them – hard. When you are stuck with an overwhelming emotion that is turning life sour, you probably are not feeling very receptive to this sagacious sentiment.

But you know what? And please don't punch me. It's true.

The intense sadness, anger, grief, or self-loathing will usually pass eventually. You will have glimmers of hope, love, or joy, even if just fleetingly. It's easy to accept that bad feeling passes when you are feeling okay or upbeat but hard to believe this when you are at your lowest ebb. But hang in there, you will feel better in the end.

But as your internal state and your circumstances change, so emotions will morph into something else. There is no point in getting too hung up on one feeling as it will change anyway. So take comfort from this, especially in times when you feel intense and difficult emotions.

How *do* you work through an overwhelming feeling without doing or saying something you will later regret?

Sometimes, especially in early sobriety, a huge, tangled mass of emotions might come up. This is normal. If you have been drinking for a long time, you will have been anesthetized from your feelings and it can be a shock to get them back in this super-concentrated form. But they *will* settle down. As you move from one sober day to the next the highs and lows will level out for most people.

Often the advice is to 'sit with' the feeling. But what does this mean? My understanding is that it means allowing the feeling to be. Recognize it, name it and be curious about it but not obsessive. For example, you might wake up feeling a bit low in energy, with a sense of doom about the day, perhaps a knot of regret or dread. By allowing the feeling, you recognize it. You might say 'I feel low' or 'I feel a sense of dread.' You don't allow it to dominate your thinking or your day. You get up. You might continue to feel all those low feelings as you go about your morning routine, but you get on with washing, eating, exercising, meditating, commuting, and working as you normally do. No need to blot out the feelings with a bottle of vodka or even ask 'why?' Just move about your day. By following the steps of a healthy morning routine, your mood will often lift a little.

You might have heard the expression 'feelings are not facts'. That doesn't mean we have to ignore feelings, judge them, squash them down, or berate ourselves for having them. Just try to be aware of the feeling without trying to immediately change it, analyze it, or completely dismiss it. I know this can be hard, especially for difficult emotions or if you feel overwhelmed, but it will help in the long term. You will learn that having a difficult feeling is okay and you don't need to panic about it or drink to soothe it. You can learn new ways to experience the feeling, respond to it and deal with it. Learning this process can take the intensity out of passing feelings.

This is how it works: First, fully experience the emotion. Where in your body do you feel it? Are you aware of any particular sets of muscles tensing up? Then name the emotion. Taking a moment or two to name the emotion can give a few seconds for the thinking, adult, rational part of your brain to respond appropriately, especially if you feel angry or hot-headed. Naming an emotion such as anger, fear, or disgust, for example, can help you to verbalize it and share your experience with someone else, often bringing relief. Phrase it as; 'I am *feeling* angry' (for example) rather than 'I am angry'. This is not playing about with words. It helps underline the fact that it is a passing feeling and not a permanent state.

Sometimes you might think you are feeling a certain emotion, but when you take a few moments to name it, you realize it is something else. For example, you might feel anger, but then when you say 'I feel angry' to yourself and you see that you actually are worried or insecure instead. This process helps get more specific.

After taking a moment to name the emotion, the next step is to treat yourself with kindness. That means accepting the feeling, not beating yourself up for experiencing it, or heaping shame on yourself. It doesn't help to think 'I shouldn't be feeling so low. I have a great spouse, lovely kids, a fantastic job...' etc. If you feel lousy, you feel lousy. Don't berate yourself for feeling what you feel. Name it, breathe....and make space for the feeling. Remember to notice in your body where you feel it. Tense shoulders, tight jaw, furrowed brow when you are angry perhaps, or feeling sick, shaky, or dizzy when you are fearful.

The next step is to do what is necessary at that moment. You can move through the day with an awareness of how you are feeling. Sometimes an emotion is fleeting and passes. After an hour absorbed in a project at work or spent running around after the kids in the park, you might think, 'Mood, what mood?' Your mood has changed, and you haven't drunk or acted out.

It has passed.

Doing what is necessary might be an act of self-care: getting a glass of water, having a nap, doing a few stretches, getting outdoors for a few minutes, calling a friend, or having a nourishing snack. The best self-care is usually simple and cheap or free.

Breathe – Take a few deep, slow breaths. So foundational, but so effective. Make a pause to breathe well, your go-to 'next right thing' when you feel overwhelmed by a negative feeling.

Sometimes we feel low and don't know why. ''*Why* am I feeling so low?'' you ask yourself over and over. Perhaps you think, reasonably, if you knew *why* you could do something about it. But sometimes we never know *why*. Sometimes it takes a while to realize why. Give yourself time to process so-called negative feelings without forcing any revelation. Relax a little. See things for what they are and let them go as best you can. Sometimes we let go and later the answer appears.

To illustrate what I mean by this process of letting go and answers appearing, consider this scenario: have you ever tried to think of a solution to a problem that just seemed to evade you as you tried harder and harder to engage your grey cells and work out an answer? Maybe something as straightforward as someone's name or a word? Or something more complex like how to approach a difficult conversation you need to have with someone? You think and think. You use reason and logic. You grit your teeth and knit your brow as you concentrate so hard that your head hurts. You give up and get on with the immediate tasks at hand. You forget about it and shrug it off. You get on with your day and that night go to sleep as usual. Then the next morning, as you surface from a deep sleep, a thought just pops into your head – the answer! That elusive and slippery name or an angle on how to approach the difficult chat you need to have just flashes across your mind.

Often that's how it is with difficult feelings. We question them. We wrestle with them, or we push them away. But they have a habit of reappearing again – and again. Or we drink, eat, or self-medicate to obliterate them. But they still lurk around, showing up as irritation, self-doubt, free-floating fear, or anxiety. However, if we give them some room without analyzing them, a thought, an image, an answer, a breakthrough happens, without us trying so hard.

When you let go you might have a revelation later. You might realize today is the anniversary of a loss or bereavement – you had consciously forgotten about it, but the deeper recesses of your mind had hung onto the memory. This memory eventually surfaced in a way your conscious mind can understand. You realize what the date is and think: 'Ahh that explains it.'

Before I close this chapter if you feel constantly very low and these methods don't help, please do get professional help.

There is more on dealing with difficult feelings in the chapter in this book called: 'Busting a Bad Mood,' so keep reading.

Summary:

- Alcohol has been acting as an anesthetic to numb out feelings. When you stop drinking you will feel your emotions more intensely.
- Make sure you are eating, hydrating, and sleeping well. Get some fresh air and exercise. Talk to other people about how you are feeling.
- Learn how to sit with a feeling, experience it, and let it go. Remember feelings will pass eventually.

Own Up and Glow Up.

"When I was drinking, I loved to watch 'Glow Up' videos. I hated my dull skin, tired puffy eyes, and stained teeth. If I could just find the right product or routine, I thought, I would have the glowing skin and bright eyes I sought. It amazed me that after a few weeks of being alcohol-free, my skin was clear, my eyes popped, and my teeth gleamed. Owning up to my drinking problem and getting sober was the best 'glow up'! I think being able to look people in the eye and smile was more effective than any treatment or technique. I could do this because I felt better about myself. I was being as honest as possible and clearing up my messes from the past. I had owned up about the problems my drinking had caused, and this gave me confidence and self-assurance I could never buy in a bottle."

Joni shared this with me via a Skype call. I could see for myself just how radiant she was.

Of course, owning up to problem drinking is only the beginning. It can be tempting to blame drinking on external events, people, or circumstances. Joni shared her struggles with recovery in the following way:

"I had a tough childhood. My father left the family home when my sisters and I were little. My mother was a heavy drinker and unable to take care of us. I tried to juggle school and look after the family. I stopped going to school when I was about 15 and I stayed at home, eventually drinking with my mom. Our lives were chaotic, and my life was a mess. My mom died of liver failure when I was in my early 20s, and the family split up. I got into an abusive relationship with a heavy drinker. For years I blamed my dad, my mom, and my ex-husband. And then when I was on my own looking at the four walls of my messy apartment, I realized there was no one to blame anymore. It was up to me. That's when I reached out for help with my drinking.''

If you have had difficulties in life, it can be so easy to pin the responsibility for drinking onto a parent, a spouse, or life in general. This means life just goes around on the same treadmill, but nothing changes. It also gives power to those other people, and you stay trapped. Owning up means taking responsibility and that decision puts the power back in your hands.

What does it look like to take responsibility?

The first step is to admit you have a problem with drinking – just own up to the consequences drinking is having in your life. A feeling of shame might push you to admit the problem, but don't let a sense of shame linger. If you have owned up to the issue, shame has done its job, so let the shame go.

It also means being accountable for your health and recovery. To do that, you can follow the plan suggested in this book and adapted it to your life. An important point in the plan is that you carry it out every day even when you don't feel like it. This is taking responsibility for yourself.

You are not doing this for anyone except yourself. Of course, other people will benefit from you being sober and happy. In the long term, though, you will stay motivated if you are doing it for yourself. If you are getting well to please a spouse and the relationship ends, you might be tempted to drink again. It puts the responsibility for your recovery onto your spouse when it needs to be with you.

Finding others to be accountable to is a powerful aid to long-term recovery. When you decide to stop drinking, tell at least one other person. This helps keep you accountable. If you have told people, you will be less inclined to give in to the temptation to drink again. You will also have someone (or ideally a few people) to call on for support and encouragement to stay alcohol-free. So, tell a trusted friend or family member who is supportive of your desire to stop drinking. You could find a therapist or coach or sponsor if you need more informed support. The person or people you are accountable to should be understanding, but not so understanding that they make excuses for you to drink or act out. They need to have the strength and honesty to call you out if you are slipping back into old behaviors.

Ultimately being accountable means showing up in life the best we can be. If you are a working professional, you will be accountable to your employer, clients, and colleagues. If you are a parent, you will be accountable to your kids. If you are not in a situation in which you are accountable to anyone or anything, find a group to be accountable to. If you join a group and keep showing up, people will get to know you. They will miss you if you drop out of attending. If you know you will have a few people asking questions about your absence at a meeting, you might think twice about drinking, so this will keep you accountable to the group. It will help you get well and stay well.

In this book, I will also encourage you to take responsibility for your Inner work (some programs call it taking a personal inventory). Most programs encourage a process of personal reflection and improvement. I will ask you to do this with an attitude of compassion and self-respect. As the book progresses, I will guide you in looking at how society has impacted you and your drinking behavior. Of course, this will vary from one woman to the next. But there are common themes that influence our attitudes toward alcohol. These may have held you back from getting well. This is not about simply blaming society, but it is about acknowledging its impact on us. I talk about this in the last section of the book. Once we know about it, we have a responsibility to do something about it for ourselves. There is no shame or blame. The inner work is simply to find out what has affected you and what to do about it to enable you to live a sober and contented life. But more on that later.

Summary:
- Stopping drinking will have many physical benefits. You will look much healthier and feel more vibrant.
- Having self-respect, confidence, and healthy esteem for yourself will give you added sparkle.
- Taking personal responsibility and being accountable are key aspects of contented and sustainable sobriety.

Part One – Summary

Part Two of the book will cover aspects of the plan in more detail. But for now, the following is a brief synopsis of the basics of the plan covered so far. In this summary, I include a reference to the chapter that relates to that part of the plan in brackets.

The Plan:

1. Have a plan. The chances of relapsing are high without a plan. (*Find Your Why?*)
   - Be clear about your 'why' – Complete your 'Purpose Statement' and keep it handy.
   - The basics of the plan are:

TREAT (What To Do)

Treat your body well

Reflect on your actions

Enjoy an activity

Absorb uplifting content

Talk to a trusted friend

2. Follow the plan every day, especially when you don't feel like it. That's when you need it most.
   - Carry out the TREAT actions every day. Create a schedule to make sure you build in time to: Treat your body well. Reflect, Enjoy a rewarding activity, Absorb uplifting or inspiring content and

Talk to a trusted friend – *every* day. *(When To Do It)*

3. Treat yourself well. Be kind to your body and mind.
   - Stop beating yourself up
   - Include activities in your daily routine that you find soothing and relaxing
   - Remember you are getting sober to enjoy life not to endure it.

4. Absorb uplifting books or audio content to keep you motivated. Read, listen or watch every day.
   - Be selective about what you watch, read, look at and listen to.
   - Focus on content that supports your efforts to be alcohol-free and makes you feel good. *(What to Do)*

5. Self-reflect and grow. Learn new skills and develop new attitudes. Be open to change.
   - Learn skills to deal with triggers to drink. Use the COPE strategy to challenge craving thoughts. *(The Most Important Distance You Will Ever Travel)*
   - Be aware of fantasy thinking. Use your imagination to visualize a sober and happy you. *(From Fantasy Island to The Land of Your Dreams)*
   - Work on changing beliefs that are holding you back from being alcohol-free. *(Swapping Out the Beer Goggles)*

6. Talk to a trusted friend or friends.

- Have a phone call or meet up with at least one trusted friend every day. Make efforts to create and maintain strong bonds with loved ones, friends and the community. (*Peeps, Pals and Playmates*)

7. Be aware of your thinking around triggers to drink and learn strategies to deal with them.
   - Use COPE to deal with craving thoughts (The Most Important Distance You Will Ever Travel)

8. Deal with disturbing emotions, whether these are from your past, present, or worries about the future.
   - Treat yourself with compassion (*Stop Beating Yourself Up*)
   - Make sure you are attending to your physical well-being – eating, moving, sleeping, hydrating and relaxing. If you have slipped into poor habits, get back to basics with *'Feel Great in 8'*: that is *8* hours of sleep portions of fruit/vegetables, 8 glasses of water, walking 8,000 steps, and for at least 8 minutes sit and do absolutely nothing. Do this every day for 8 days and see if your moods improve.
   - Keep track of your moods and consider how they relate to hormonal fluctuations due to menstruation, perimenopause, menopause, or other factors. Get a medical check-up if your moods don't improve after making some basic improvements to your lifestyle.

- Learn to experience emotions, let them run their course, and know they will pass, no matter how intense. *(Getting Your Feelings Back)*

9. Enjoy an activity you like as a reward every day. Play and take pleasure in life.
   - People who build in regular rewards and small treats are more motivated to get sober and stay that way.
   - Build in time to play and enjoy life

The content in the chapters in the next part of the book gives you much more detail on how to carry out the 9-point plan, so keep reading.

PART
TWO.

How Are You Coping?

Remember in Part One of the book there is a chapter called *'The Most Important Distance You Will Ever Travel'*? In that chapter, I talked about craving thoughts and how to deal with them. I also introduced the COPE strategy and encouraged you to categorize your thoughts as *Compulsive, Opportunity, Promise,* or *Emotional*.

Because cravings are so persistent and can be so destructive to recovery, I include more strategies here to give you support in overcoming them. They often hit when you feel most vulnerable and can be hard to resist. So, if craving thoughts are undermining your best intentions to stay sober, read on.

If you have a troubling thought that is urging you to drink, my first tip is to *take your body somewhere else and your head will follow*. Let me explain. When we have a strong urge to do something we don't want to do, we can end up doing mental gymnastics. We get into a 'push/pull' argument in our heads. We can get wrapped up in these thoughts, so move your body somewhere else. If we stay by the source of temptation, we can start to rationalize drinking. The mental contortions can be crazy-making. The anxiety that builds up about drinking/not drinking makes us more vulnerable to giving in. And what do we often do if we are anxious? Yep, take a drink. So, take yourself away from the anxiety-causing situation and calm down. *Take your body somewhere else and your head will follow*. There is a chance that when you move physically from the source of temptation, your mind will calm down and the mental somersaults will stop. It's simple but effective. You can't drink the booze if you can't physically reach it. So, remove yourself physically.

The next method coming up is best used when you have walked away from the source of temptation. This strategy involves using the power of your imagination. Imagine you are holding a flashlight. Picture the flashlight in your hand and see yourself shining the light at what is right in front of you at that moment. Point that flashlight at the task in hand or the person in front of you. The flashlight is your attention and focus. For example, if you are at work, intensely concentrate on what you are doing. If you are working at a computer screen, read every word carefully and slowly. If you are talking to someone, use your imaginary flashlight to light up their face, and focus on the expression in their eyes, their body language, or details about their appearance. If you are relaxing, say, watching a movie, concentrate on the storyline, acting and scenery in the film as if your life depends on it. Shift your full attention away from the thought of a drink and shine it on what is in front of you. Often, your mind gets absorbed by the work, the conversation, or the action in the movie and forgets about the random thought that has passed through your mind.

When you are feeling low and emotional, craving thoughts can be especially difficult to deal with. Recurrent emotional thoughts might mean you need to find something else to soothe yourself other than alcohol if you feel low or sad. This book has lots of ideas on dealing with bad moods. If low moods, sad feelings, or loneliness are major triggers for you, put together a list of things to do that provide you with the comfort you need. When we are in the midst of blue feelings, it is easy to forget about simple pleasures that can lift us, such as a cheerful playlist of music on your phone, looking at happy photos of your family, partner, or pet, watching inspiring or funny videos, phoning a friend for a chat, reading a book purely for pleasure, or a hot beverage. These are just some ideas.

The point here is to be prepared.

Sooner or later, you will experience a mood that will drive you to seek a drink. It might be a low mood or a feeling of celebration. After all, this is what your brain has learned to do in reaction to certain emotions. So be ready for it.

If you tend to drink when you feel down, make a list of five or six of your favorite activities to turn to when you feel this way. Keep the list handy, perhaps as a note on your phone or file on your PC. Make the list when you feel calm and cheerful so you can turn to it when needed. I would urge you to make that list now.

This seems like such a simple idea, but Casey's experience illustrates how powerful it can be. She read a draft of this chapter and shared the following with me on how this strategy helped her:

''I was resistant to the idea of making a list. It seems boring, and I think of myself as a spontaneous person. But I knuckled down and made my list. I'm a hands-on type of gal, so I took the list idea a step further and collected together a variety of objects that help me feel calmer and happier. I spent an evening cleaning out an ottoman at home. It was filled with junk. I replaced the junk with a fluffy fleece blanket, some incense sticks, a candle and matches, and my favorite type of tea. I go to the ottoman if I am alone and feel lonely. As soon as I open the box and inhale the perfume from the incense, I begin to feel more relaxed. I then make some tea, light a candle, and snuggle up in the blanket. It always makes me feel better.''

Perhaps, you are tempted to drink during a special occasion. If you have thoughts that suggest an opportunity to drink. You might feel compelled to give in to it simply because the opportunity is there, maybe at a party or while out with friends. So, if a chance comes up to drink and your craving is telling you it will be different this time or that having a drink is a great idea, try this hack: *fast-forward the video*. This involves using your imagination, just like I encouraged you to do in the chapter called, *From Fantasy Island to the Land of Your Dreams*. Imagine you are watching a video of yourself taking that drink. This means in your mind's eye. Picture what will happen next if you do have that drink. How will it end up? How does it *usually* end up? Use your imagination to fill in lots of detail. How will you look, what will you say, what sorts of things will you do when you've had a drink or two or more?

If you want to use something really easy, try this super simple strategy: *Do 30 Things*. That means doing 30 things but counting each small activity. As soon as the thought hits you, count all the next small actions you take until you reach 30. For example, wash your hands – count 1. Wipe the kitchen tops – count 2. Water a plant – count

3. Empty the dishwasher – count 4, and continue to 30. If you lose count, go back to 1. Doing this will give time for the thought to pass. I have used this strategy myself to deal with all sorts of cravings. At one point in my life, I had the phrase *'Do 30 Things'* on post-it notes at home and in my work diary. It distracted me from the craving and also made me super-productive at home and work!

The next tip is more of a mind hack. Craving thoughts will make all sorts of false promises and tell all sorts of lies. One of the biggest and most dangerous lies that might urge you to drink is this one – I call it the ''Forever Thought''. Thoughts like *"I will feel like this forever"* or *"I will never have fun again."* This type of thought tells you that you will feel this bad forever.

You won't.

It might feel rough today but if you hang in there and don't lift a drink, you *will* feel better. If you do drink, you are just jumping back onto the alcohol rollercoaster. You'll do another loop and end up crashing back down again. So, keep your feet on firm ground.

So, the last thought to leave you with is *"**never** forever"*

If you think *"I can never have a drink again."* That means you will be grappling with the idea of ''forever''. That is a long time. Too long for any of us to wrap our heads around. So just keep your mind fixed on the day at hand. 'Forever' will take care of itself.

For now, to make the ideas in this chapter work in your life you need to pause this moment. Bring to mind the types of craving thoughts you usually have. Consider the strategies in this chapter. Which ones are most useful to you? Now pick one strategy. Review it and commit it to memory. Next, take action such as writing a list or preparing a box of objects like Casey did with her ottoman full of goodies to help soothe herself when she feels low. Be prepared so that when a craving thought hits you, you will be ready for it.

There are more methods to deal with these types of thoughts on the WinsPress.com website under the tab 'Free Stuff.' So, take a look there for some additional ideas. Also, my book *Mindfulness for Alcohol Recovery*, co-authored with Lewis David, is full of ideas on coping with these types of cravings. Details of the book are also on the WinsPress.com website.

Summary:

- Cravings are normal and natural. By being prepared for them, you can give yourself the best chances of success in overcoming cravings.
- You can *mentally* prepare yourself by learning strategies such as using your imagination by fast-forwarding the video or using the flashlight to hyper-focus on the task. You can prepare yourself *practically* by putting together a list or box full of items to calm, relax or distract you when you feel an urge to drink.
- Choose one strategy now and prepare yourself *mentally* and/or *practically* so that you can deal successfully with the craving when it hits.

Grab a Flashlight.

We can feel like we are lurching about in a dark room when we drink heavily. We might see vague shadows and try to move around them, only to bump into something else. We crash from one obstacle to another. Life feels hard and we can't make sense of what is going on. We are just hurt and bruised.

When we stop drinking, it can feel like the light is pouring in, showing up all those shadowy objects in our way. Some things we see clearly, and the 'a-ha' moments stack up. Some other things stay in the shadow, and we continue to hurt ourselves on them. This hurt can show up as flashes of irrational anger, resentment about the past, fear, self-loathing, or depression. Working through these feelings is essential. If we don't do this, we will probably drink again.

When we put the drink down, buried feelings will come to the surface. Being alcohol-free gives us more awareness. This can be unsettling. But instead of panicking and reaching for a drink, see this experience as a sign of progress. The flashlight of awareness can feel like a bright light coming on after you've been in darkness for a long time. The light can make you squint and hurt your eyes, but that doesn't make the light a bad thing. It is a matter of adjusting and focusing.

Of course, this newfound emotional sensitivity in early sobriety is not confined to women. Everyone struggles with issues such as regret, grudges, self-reproach, or the effects of some form of trauma. But in addition to the regular slings and arrows of life, women have also inherited the burden of misogyny. Misogyny in our culture shows up as attacks on women and continued inequality.

Women face unrealistic expectations. Many women spoke to me about the unrealistic demands for perfection that society places upon them – expectations of an immaculate home, pristine children, amazing personal appearance, accomplishments, and career success. The mismatch between reality and expectations can eat away at our self-esteem. We might have critical thoughts about ourselves. We might not question them or even be aware of them. They might just lurk about in the background, undermining self-respect and esteem.

Look at how women are portrayed in the media, on TV, in newspapers, or listen to the lyrics of some popular songs. Look at the images in magazines and on the internet. How are women presented? Girls and women absorb these societal messages. This cultural pollution has an enormous impact on girls and women. In particular in how girls and women perceive themselves.

If someone is routinely told they are less important, deserve less power, and are judged by how they look, dress, and show up in the world, it is abusive. This low-level, daily psychological bashing is damaging. No wonder many women are depressed, anxious, and drinking due to feelings of shame, unacceptability, and feeling 'less than'. You might be unaware of these feelings when you drink heavily. But when you stop, they can come crashing in.

Alternatively, you might well have a period of euphoria when you stop drinking – especially when you start to feel better physically – with an upsurge of good feelings. Ex-drinkers often call it a 'pink cloud'. But then the pink cloud dissipates. This is when some difficult feelings might come to the surface.

Don't worry. This is perfectly normal. Whether the feelings hit you in the first few days of stopping drinking or they take a while to surface, don't panic. Instead, see this situation as an opportunity to be patient, kind, and loving with yourself. These so-called negative emotions are probably an indication that something is ready to be released, be freed. So let it filter up into your awareness. Resist the urge to push the feelings away with alcohol, food, compulsive behavior, or old habits. Recognize them as just feelings – significant indicators of what is going on in your world, but signs pointing you in a new direction.

In the last chapter, we discussed the analogy of a flashlight giving you focus and awareness. And, bit by bit, this flashlight of awareness shows up the true situation you were unaware of before. This takes the power out of those situations from the past holding you back – perhaps memories, flashbacks, resentments or hurts from your earlier life. But when we see things for how they are – like the Wizard of Oz being shown up as a little old man behind a curtain – they lose their power.

For example, if you are feeling a vague sense of discontent with yourself, use your flashlight to see this as a reaction to the barrage of images of 'perfect' women you have been assailed by as you watch TV. You do not need to rush off to get a nose job or down a bottle of vodka to blur the 'unacceptable' image you see in the mirror. With awareness, you see that you have just been needlessly comparing yourself to some fantasy images, and criticism and discontent have crept in, undermining your self-esteem.

Many women drink to deal with the effects of direct trauma, using alcohol as an anesthetic to subdue the pain. There are direct and clear links between trauma and addiction. If trauma has happened as a child, modern neurology and brain scans show how the experience has affected the development of the brain. Traumatized people are neurologically more inclined to get addicted. That is how their brains are wired.

Trauma is a massive factor in why some women start to drink and carry-on drinking, even when they want to stop. The statistics indicate that women are likely to have suffered traumatic experiences in the form of abuse, assault, or sexual attack. At the very least we will have been exposed to deprecating and insulting messages about what it means to be a female by what we see all around us.

You might think the symptoms of trauma are limited to disturbing flashbacks or memories. But trauma symptoms can show up as habits you have dismissed as personality traits. Habits such as constant busyness and not feeling safe enough just to 'be'.

Perhaps you push yourself hard physically. Often, people who have suffered trauma feel a disconnect from their bodies. Many women report feeling like this, disassociating from their physical selves as they push themselves into exercise when they are exhausted, or carrying on working when they need to rest. Being fiercely independent can be seen as a positive trait, but if the thought of relying on another person for help or support terrifies you, it could be a sign of trauma.

Are you constantly chasing novel information, searching endlessly for the right book or guru or course that will help you rather than looking inwards and following your wisdom and intuition? Do you find it hard to accept praise or success? Do you feel like an imposter if you are seen as an expert in your field or recognized for your achievements? Are you constantly doubting yourself? These traits could indicate that trauma is affecting your feelings and how you relate to the world. If you think you might be suffering from the effects of trauma, I urge you to seek support from a qualified professional.

Many of the women I spoke to in researching for this book reported feeling a sense of just not being *good* enough. 'Good' could stand for clever, pretty, thin, fit, cheerful, accomplished, and so on. For some, there was a low-level sensation of being insufficient, incomplete, or just plain bad. For others, there was pain, about the mistakes they had made in the past or the actions they had taken whilst under the influence of alcohol. Unfortunately, we can't turn the clock back and re-run those situations. So how do we deal with these challenging feelings, emotions, and memories, without lifting a drink?

Talking these issues through with a trusted friend, sponsor or counselor can benefit hugely. Look at your part in the situation and decide how best you can put it right as you move forward. As you look back at your past learn from it and decide how best to proceed. Identify any patterns or recurring mistakes and focus on these areas to work on as you move forward. If you need to pay back a debt, make an apology or repair a damaged relationship, do that.

And move on. Do what you can do and *let the situation go*.

We all have aspects of our past, our behavior, our actions, thoughts, or choices that cause us shame. Everyone has done or said things they regret. If you fall into a period of regret or self-reproach, treat yourself as if you were supporting and encouraging a much-loved friend or child. If your friend or child made a mistake, you wouldn't yell at them and tell them how stupid they are, you would encourage and support them. Perhaps help them make realistic plans to avoid making the same error in the future. So do the same for yourself. You messed up in the past. Who hasn't? Every human being on this planet has made mistakes or taken actions they have later regretted. So, give yourself a break. This is being compassionate towards yourself.

Be compassionate with yourself every single day. Some things you do every day, like brushing your teeth or showering. You know you need to do these things every day. They are just part of your routine. So shower yourself with self-compassion every day. Choose to let go not just of the booze but let go of beating yourself up too.

You have let go of alcohol and now you can start to let go of any self-loathing, shame, or guilt that flashlight of awareness is showing up. Encourage yourself, surround yourself with positive supportive people, and get involved in a recovery circle, or a group that lifts you. Do what you can do to repair the damage from the past, then let it go and move on.

Perhaps your flashlight has shown up someone else's behavior. Feelings of anger or resentment might come to the surface. At some point, you will need to forgive and let go. This does not mean you *forget* about it and nor does it mean that what has happened is insignificant. It means you are forgiving the person to attain freedom for yourself. Even just being willing to forgive is a good start. By deciding that you will forgive, you will be getting closer to freedom from the hold that person or situation has over you.

Talk it through with someone you trust. Talking about it or sharing it with a trusted friend or group helps in the process. It is best to find someone or a group of people who will not give you advice, just listen.

Write down what happened. If the person who inflicted pain on you is dead, write them a letter telling them how you feel and that you are deciding to forgive them. You are taking back control. Even just deciding to forgive someone can help. You don't need to force anything. You don't need to feel loving or forgiving. Just use your will to make a conscious choice to release the power the person or situation has over you. If the memories are overwhelmingly painful or traumatic, do get professional support.

The point is to keep offloading all those dark, heavy feelings that have been weighing you down. You can do this by talking them through, writing about them, and getting the right level of support, whether that is an informal group or a professional counselor or therapist.

Remember, letting go of shame, hurt, anger and self-loathing is a process. Putting down the alcohol is the first step in the process. You are letting go of all the poison that has thwarted your growth – the poison of harsh criticism, hatred, reproach, or negativity aimed at yourself or others.

If you have pain that comes up from the past, you can be the caring adult who takes care of you. Perhaps you never learned skills of self-care or self-soothing. Learn to take care of yourself and how to calm and soothe yourself. Practical, cheap ways to soothe yourself are warm baths, snuggly blankets, a self-massage, a foot rub, or asking a friend or loved one to massage your neck and shoulders. Instead of material gifts for your birthday gift, suggest vouchers for a professional massage or reflexology session. If you are on a budget, you could approach a college in which students offer these services for free or vastly reduced as they hone their skills. Physical methods such as these, help integrate and calm the nervous system. So even if money and time are short, you can still find ways to incorporate these physical therapies into your life.

Going forward, I want to encourage you to build up your self-esteem and self-confidence. To help you do that before we end this chapter, take a few moments to consider what you value in your life - grab your flashlight and let it light up *your* values. What qualities do you admire in other people? What *character traits* are you most proud of in yourself? Do you value robust health, challenging work, and being dependable or trustworthy? Be clear about your values and align your actions with them.

By 'align your actions' I mean pick out one or two aspects of life that are important to you. Consider if your actions match up with what you value. Do your actions help or damage these valued parts of your life? For example, if you value honesty, do you routinely tell small lies? If so, be as honest as you can and you will feel more pride in yourself. If you value being a good parent, prioritize your relationship with your kids – listen to them, play with them, and take an interest in what is important to them. By lining up what you do with what you value, you don't need to reproach yourself and shame doesn't rear its ugly head so often.

So, look at the first few days, weeks, and months of sobriety as a period of transition. You are in transition from that drunken person stumbling about in a dark room to the empowered woman holding the flashlight. You can now throw light on the cultural messages, people, resentments, memories, or trauma that have been tripping you up and hurting you.

The flashlight is in your hands.

Summary:

- When we stop drinking, we feel all the emotions we have been numbing with alcohol. These difficult feelings can come from our past actions, what has happened to us, and also from the effects of the culture we live in. If we don't work on these issues, we might drink excessively again.
- We can deal with these feelings by talking to others, writing about how we feel, forgiving ourselves and others, and putting things right as best we can. We can soothe ourselves with physical therapies to feel more comfortable.
- We can work on becoming more aware of what we value in life and line up our actions with our values. By doing this we can move forward with more confidence, assurance, and healthy self-esteem.

Bouncing Back.

No doubt your health, finances, work-life, and relationships will improve when you become alcohol-free. But life goes on after you decide to stop drinking. The stresses that perhaps fuelled your drinking will still be there to some degree. New challenges will inevitably come along. That's life. A key aspect of staying sober is learning to cope with those stresses. In addition, you will learn how to overcome triggers that might prompt you to lift a drink again.

The ability to bounce back when life throws a curveball is essential for happy long-term sobriety. This is called resilience. Resilience is not grit-your-teeth toughness, but it does mean you can adapt to difficult life circumstances. It means working through difficulties without resorting to a drink. It means being able to solve problems, cope with stress and feel optimistic about life. If you constantly feel overwhelmed and defeated, your sobriety will be undermined. Cultivating resilience is a superpower in overcoming stress and the temptation to drink.

Maybe you are unsure of how strong your resilience is at the moment. Resilience is a big topic and can be confusing. If someone tells us we need to be more resilient, what does this mean? And how resilient are you already?

To help you work this out I have devised *The Resilience Tracker*. I have broken up the topic of resilience into the following sections of specific personal skills:

- Self-awareness
- Meaning and purpose
- Problem-solving and dealing with stress
- Being realistic about life
- Growth and development

Now we will look at each section and explore what that particular skill involves. I will prompt you to give yourself a rating on how well you feel you can apply each aptitude to your life. If you struggle with a skill your score will be closer to 0. If you feel you are strong in that area, give yourself a score closer to 10. There is no shame or blame here. The score is just for you. The purpose of doing this is for two reasons: firstly, to help you nail down exactly how you can grow your resilience, and secondly, to chart your progress. You can return to the resilience tracker exercise later and complete this again. Your results will help you to focus on areas that need improvement in a very specific way. So now let's look at each aspect of resilience and explore what it means and how you can improve.

If you find it difficult to score yourself at this point, that's okay. In the next chapter I discuss what the results might look like in real life, so read that and come back to the exercise. In the next chapter, I also give specific actions to help build resilience. But for now, let's look at each aspect of resilience and get started.

1. Self-awareness - do you feel you are in touch with your thoughts and feelings?

Being aware of thoughts and feelings isn't airy-fairy. Identifying types of thoughts and feelings can help you keep a level head and make decisions in line with your choices. This ability will help avoid spiraling down towards a drink. If you spot the early signs of a low mood, for example, you can take pre-emptive action such as talking with a friend or taking some time out to take stock of what is going well in your life. For some people, being on a high can be a trigger to drink. There are lots of ideas on becoming aware of moods promptly in the chapter in this book called *How to Bust a Bad Mood*.

If you tend to push troubling thoughts away quickly or are only aware of a feeling when you lose control and snap at someone or dissolve into tears, give yourself a score closer to zero and mark this as an area to work on. Many of the chapters in part of this book give you guidance on building awareness of thoughts and feelings, including the chapters called: The *Most Important Distance You Will Ever Travel, Swapping Out the Beer Goggles,* and *Getting Your Feelings Back.* If this is an area you have highlighted as the one you want to work on, go back and re-read the chapters and apply some of these suggestions. Use your reflection time each day to check on how you are progressing in this area.

2. Do you have a strong sense of purpose and meaning in your life?

Earlier in the book, I asked you to think about your purpose in getting sober. But, if you haven't done it already, pause now and take a moment to clarify in your mind what *your* meaning and purpose in getting sober is. Being clear about why you have stopped drinking can help keep you motivated when things go wrong. What has motivated you to make the necessary changes to become alcohol-free? Health? Finances? A relationship? Children? Recall the defining moment you decided enough was enough. Perhaps it was serious news from the doctor or the risk of losing your kids. Your purpose might change over time, so it is worth reviewing it regularly to avoid complacency or stagnation.

If you are still rather vague about your purpose give yourself a lower score and go back to the chapter in Part 1 of this book called *Find Your Why* to help clarify your purpose. Alternatively, if you have your purpose sentence all prepared and you are very clear about your 'why', score yourself closer to 10.

You might remember Janine who we met in the first section of this book. Janine used a vision board as a way to record her purpose. She pasted attractive pictures of people walking in lovely places to inspire herself to get outdoors to move. To encourage herself to eat better she pinned up her favorite recipes. Janine's visual reminder also helped her to remember to respond to her own basic needs. Attending to basic physical needs is foundational to building a healthy resilience. So having a clear purpose for self-care may give you the motivation you need to look after yourself if you are the type of person to put your needs last. You need to feel as healthy, fit, and vibrant as possible to build a resilient and enjoyable life free from alcohol.

3. Problem-solving. Can you live with a problem you can't solve yet? Are you confident about solving problems in your life?

Many of us have problems and issues in life that we can't solve directly or not yet. Perhaps a difficult boss, a stressful job, or an unruly teenager at home. Living with a difficult issue or problem requires patience, resourcefulness, and the ability to deal with the stress the issue causes. This is being resilient. We met Janine earlier, she shared with me how having a clear sense of purpose helped her, she also discussed with me her strategies for dealing with her job which I share with you next.

Janine's job presents her with constant challenges. Working as a nurse, she has a lot of in-the-moment pressure. These pressures include dealing with emergencies and making quick decisions to prioritize her caring duties. Janine was keen to share with me her methods to deal with this 'in-your-face stress' as she calls it. When dealing with these situations, Janine focuses on her breathing, she breathes in for 7 and out for 11. She can do this as she gets on with the job at hand. The other go-to strategy she shared with me is centered on her physical body: she quickly tightens up all her muscles, holds for a couple of seconds, and then lets go. Also, Janine now takes the opportunity to talk through her feelings at work with colleagues and her Charge Nurse.

These practices are simple and easy. But the difference for Janine is that she *does* them. She laughs:

"Before I got sober, as a nurse, I knew what I should be doing for my mental well-being, but my idea of stress relief was getting off the ward as soon as possible and hitting the nearest bar. Now, I take time to talk through what has happened during my shift over a coffee at handover, cycle home and cook myself a nice meal. I can't tell you how much peace of mind this gives me. No more 4 a.m. wakeups, worrying about my dodgy decisions at work. I sleep with a clear conscience."

Before Janine developed her skills to deal with the challenges her job presents, she would have had a low score for this question. Janine previously found it difficult to live with issues she could not immediately solve and the stress this created pushed her towards the nearest bar. Nowadays with her effective methods for managing her stress, she would score highly. These stress-management skills have helped her to be more resilient and avoid drinking.

4. Do you feel that you think realistically about your life? Do you feel optimistic about life?

Many of us can fall into a trap of black-and-white thinking. Being realistic about life does not necessarily mean looking at the gloomier side of life, nor is being realistic the opposite of being optimistic. It is possible to be *realistically optimistic*. Being realistically optimistic helps you become more resilient and avoids the type of all-or-nothing thinking that can lead to a drink. Let me explain.

To illustrate what I mean, let's look at the experiences of another woman, Amy, whom I spoke to while researching this book. Amy shared with me what she did to become more resilient. She presents as a smiling, fresh-faced millennial. Rosy-cheeked from a dog walk with her black lab, Monty, she exudes cheerfulness and is quick to laugh at the antics of her dog as she greets me. Amy explained how things had been for her. She worked from home, was single and her only responsibility was her dog, who she doted on. Amy had an administrative role for an events company and her stresses would ebb and flow according to how busy the company was. Amy takes a moment to reflect on her recent past, her face darkening a little as she sighed and continued:

" My daily routine constituted work, drink, pass out, repeat. Luckily, I worked at home, and if I logged onto my work account and appeared active, nobody asked too many questions. Poor Monty usually had to make do with moping about in the garden while I attempted to work or slept off the vodka from the night before. I ordered food online and avoided people as much as possible. I had no joy in anything and constantly complained to anyone who would listen. I tried to get sober before, but it didn't last long. Nothing changed and I still complained and felt sorry for myself because I am on my own.

It's a funny thing, I still have the same life – the same job, the same house, and everything. But I feel so different about it all and I am happy to be alcohol-free. A major mind shift for me this time was learning about 'optimistic realism'. My doctor gave me an NHS leaflet about it. I used to hate anything that reeked of 'positivity'. I prided myself on being realistic and quite cynical really. I didn't want to pretend everything was fine when it wasn't. But optimistic realism helped me. Nowadays I can see the good stuff in my life and don't feel the need to drink because I'm feeling low or sad."

Amy touched on the problem of simply trying to be 'positive'. There are lots of advantages to adopting a cheerful outlook, but without awareness and honesty, it can be easy to feel pressured into forcing a smile or a jolly outlook when you don't feel that way. Realistic optimism means seeing things as they are and deciding to maintain a constructive outlook on life whilst being aware of the difficulties. It's also about taking responsibility for choices and actions and looking at solutions rather than getting bogged down in the problems. I am aware that realistic optimism is a key skill in developing and maintaining resilience, so I was keen for Amy to expand on exactly what she had done to nurture this essential tool. When I questioned Amy further on this aspect of her sobriety, she had this to say:

"Before I got sober, I was just drifting really, I often felt sorry for myself. My parents are divorced, my dad lives in Australia and my mum passed away ten years ago when I was just 20. I felt very alone. I was at art college when she died, and I had left the course to look after her.

When the doctors could do nothing more for her, I retreated into my shell and felt incredibly angry at the world. I lost touch with friends, and I became very isolated. I found it oddly comforting to prefer anything dark. You name it: zombie movies, horror novels, and I preferred music with morbid lyrics. I just existed really. I kept thinking about how meaningless my life was. Having Monty to care for was the only thing that kept me going. I pride myself on being a realist but when I stopped drinking, even I could see how my interests and lifestyle weren't helping me, so I went to the doctor to talk about my low feelings and got into this realistic optimism thing. I realized that I can either choose to look at my life as a disaster, which it isn't, or choose to see it more realistically as having some bad bits to deal with and some good things too, like my house, my job, and Monty. I made a few changes too, such as joining a dog agility club that gets me out and I have joined a few online support groups to get support to stay sober. I just have this feeling now that I can cope with the difficult stuff and I'm not on my own in a lonely way. I like being in my own company, I'm a bit of an introvert but I am learning to get out and mix too, which has defiantly helped"

Amy hit on two aspects of resilience that need to be highlighted. One was her observation that she could *choose* to look at her life negatively or in a more upbeat light. She chose the latter and as a result felt more cheerful about her circumstances. Second, Amy learned to reach out to others for companionship and support. Even though Amy is a self-defined introvert, these connections added a missing dimension to her life and lifted her out of her isolation.

Amy had developed skills in being more realistically optimistic and would now score highly in this area of the resilience questionnaire.

5. Do you feel like you can do new things to grow and develop?

Having a sense of growth and development ties in with feeling optimistic about the future. We all can grow, learn new skills, and develop. This is not about intelligence, particular attributes, or talents. It is simply about a mindset that says you can learn new stuff and keep evolving as a human being. Everyone can do this. Sometimes we just forget.

The fact that you have read this far into the book and hopefully tried out some of the exercises and suggestions shows clearly that you have the motivation and tenacity to grow and develop. So notch up that score and give yourself some praise. Keep reading, as this book will give you many more ideas on how to continue to grow and develop.

How did you score? Have you thought about each section and decided how you are doing right now? Here is a summary of the sections I have highlighted in the resilience tracker, for you to score yourself:

- Self-awareness
- Meaning and purpose
- Problem-solving and dealing with stress
- Being realistic about life
- Growth and development

Think about each heading and out of 10 decide where you are at. A low score indicates you need to give more attention to that area to be more resilient. I worked through this myself today and my lowest score was on problem-solving, especially dealing with problems I don't have a solution for yet, so this is an area I will work on personally to increase my resilience.

If you have had difficulty scoring yourself, don't worry. In the next chapter I describe what a low, average, or high score looks like in real life, so read that and come back to the exercise when you feel ready.

Breaking the huge area of resilience up into these headings helps to focus on the particular area that is most in need of attention. Work on one area at a time. Repeat this exercise regularly to keep developing your resilience. You will remember 'R' stands for *reflection* in the memory aid 'TREAT'. You could complete your resilience tracker exercise as part of your reflection time.

In the next chapter, I discuss what your score tells you about yourself. I also discuss more ways to build your strength, feel better about life, and stay away from the booze. So keep reading.

Summary:

- Resilience is all about bouncing back when life gets tough. It is a life skill that can be learned and practiced.
- Key aspects of resilience are having a well-defined purpose in getting and staying sober, being self-aware, dealing effectively with problems, being realistically optimistic about life, and knowing you can grow and develop.
- The resilience tracker exercise in this chapter will help you work out what you need to work on to become more resilient. Redo the exercise at regular intervals to chart your progress.

Your Resilience Results.

So, how did you do?

If you completed the exercise in the last chapter, you have a set of scores. This is for your information to help you grow resilience skills. These skills will help you to stop drinking and get more out of life, so it is worth spending some time on them.

If you haven't done the exercise yet, that's okay. If you aren't sure how to score yourself, read through this chapter and go back and complete it.

So, in the following paragraphs, I discuss what your scores might mean and what they might look like in real life. Also, I give you some ideas on how you can develop your skills in each aspect of resilience.

I band the scores into a 'low' score of 0 – 3, an 'average' score of 4 – 7, and a 'high' score of 8 – 10. You can look at your results, read the paragraphs that are relevant to your score, or read this chapter straight through. The important thing is that you take away at least one key practice to action when you finish reading. I summarize the key practices at the end of each section in this chapter.

But let's move on to see what your scores reveal about you.

Self-awareness.
Low (0 – 3)

You have thoughts and feelings that seem to creep up on you and explode out of nowhere. You can be suddenly beset by deep sadness or gripped by intense desire without any apparent build-up to it.

Other people might describe you as impulsive. Perhaps you are the sort of person who goes shopping and arrives home with all sorts of odd purchases you did not intend to buy. These impulse purchases might include alcohol.

At times you might be bewildered by other people's reactions towards you or have a vague sense of upsetting someone but not knowing why. Arguments with other people seem to blow up out of nowhere and you find yourself snapping at people when you don't want to.

Any form of criticism, even constructive feedback, makes you feel sick with self-doubt, and you blow up angrily if anyone dares to question your work or behavior.

Time alone is boring for you. If you find yourself on your own, you can slip into feeling lonely and sorry for yourself. This can act as a trigger to drink.

You might be a very motivated person and you push yourself towards exhaustion, unwilling to take a break. Perhaps you take on too much or jump from project to project. You then end up feeling overworked and resentful, so you drink to unwind.

Average (4 – 7)

When life is fairly calm you can spot feelings building up and identify patterns of thinking that you know will lead to trouble. You might take pre-emptive action to improve a low mood or challenge your thoughts that you know will bring down your feelings of well-being. However, when life gets a bit crazy, you might get caught up in the storm and forget to check in on yourself. That's when you are most at risk of drinking even if you have decided not to.

You might occasionally be surprised by someone's reactions towards you or puzzled by their behavior in a relationship. You might find it difficult to accept feedback or any form of criticism in a constructive way. You might take it to heart and over-compensate, working extra hard to improve things outside of your responsibility. This can lead to you feeling resentful. Resentment can often push us towards a drink.

Alternatively, you might feel defensive when any form of criticism comes your way. You might find yourself worrying about what other people think of you and try to alter your behavior to fit in with their expectations.

You are quite focused on the external world and find it a bit boring or selfish to spend time looking at your thoughts and feelings.

High (8 – 10)

If you have given yourself a high score in the area of self-awareness, you know that perfection is not part of the deal. You don't think in black and white terms and accept that life is more of a zig-zag and not a continuous upward line towards the angelic.

On the whole, you are open to feedback from others and see your mistakes and slip-ups as opportunities for learning. You are keen to find out more about yourself and how you relate to others and the world.

You enjoy time alone and like to read, journal, or follow a spiritual practice.

During busy periods you can carve out a few moments here and there to tune into your bodily sensations and feelings. You can feel emotions as they build from a small niggle or sensation, and you take a moment to feel it and perhaps question it.

You look at life with deep interest and rarely feel bored. Your thoughts, feelings, and reactions are sources of feedback giving you information about how you are engaging with the world. You take time to breathe and fully experience what is going on around you and how you feel internally. This is almost second nature to you. You have a habitual practice of reviewing your day each evening.

No matter how you have scored, there is always room for improvement in this area. None of us can be one hundred percent self-aware. Even if you scored 10, there will be aspects of your feelings, thoughts, and interactions that are not yet apparent to you. We all have our blind spots.

To build self-awareness, you can develop a practice of regularly checking in with yourself. By this I mean, taking a nano-second to be aware of what you are feeling. No need to analyze it. Just name it. For example, *"Right now I feel contented"*. That's how I feel right now.

It's raining outside, I've been for a walk, had breakfast, and am happy to get on with some work. I am physically comfortable. There is nothing particularly exciting going on today but neither have I had any bad news or disappointment. So, I feel contented.

An especially helpful time to take a moment to look at how you are feeling is when you start to feel a challenging emotion build, especially if you feel attacked by what someone has just said. Take a moment to be curious about te feeling rather than launch into a counter-attack right away. Look at your reactions. When you feel under attack, do you want to fight? Or do you freeze or want to run away? Being aware of your reactions gives you valuable insight into how you habitually deal with difficult feelings or confrontations. You can then decide calmly how you would like to handle them and act with intention. In the meantime, the encounter has given you some information about how you habitually respond. This is part of self-awareness.

Key practices to improve self-awareness:

- Do regular check-ins. Ask yourself, 'How am I feeling?'
- Take a moment here and there during the day to look at the thoughts running through your mind.
- Get into a habit of reviewing your day each evening.

Meaning and Purpose.

Low (0 – 3)

You might feel low-level hopelessness or a sense of *'what's the use?'* Your purpose in getting sober is probably based on what other people want or expect of you.

You might feel like a victim of other people's behavior. Life might seem random, chaotic, and cruel. Perhaps you struggle with poor health or poverty. These are real problems and I empathize with you. I have felt these feelings in those types of circumstances. I grew up in difficult circumstances, with limited opportunities, no money, and parents with their own significant problems. Life can be hard. But even in the darkest of times, there will be meaning and purpose. Even if your only purpose is to get through the day without drinking, that is a purpose. You can gently build on that. If your health, finances, or relationships are wrecked through drinking, then getting sober and healthy is your purpose. Focus on getting well and give yourself some kudos for reading this book and making the effort to get better.

Average (4 – 7)

Most days you have a sense of purpose. Your motivation to get and stay sober is fairly consistent. However, there might be days when it all wavers. You might question yourself or feel sabotaged by other people's behavior. For example, you decide to go to a recovery meeting, but your husband forgets and takes the car, arriving home too late for you to get to your meeting. So be clear and firm with others about what you need to help you stick to your purpose to avoid getting derailed.

Your off-days might be due to low mood, poor health, or bad luck. Start with the basics and address any health concerns, make sure you eat well, get enough sleep, and have time to do things you enjoy. Build in rewards for your continued sobriety. Make your purpose worthwhile for *you*.

High (8 – 10)

Wow! You are so motivated you might be a bit scary to be around! You are perhaps a very driven person in most areas of life, and now you have discovered the benefits of sobriety, you are a force to be reckoned with. Your sense of purpose is of huge benefit to you in terms of resilience, nothing much gets you off track from your goal of being alcohol-free. You see challenges as opportunities to grow and develop. Temper this enthusiasm with empathy for the struggles of other people. Later in the book, I talk about the need for balance, so look at that section carefully to ensure your sense of meaning and purpose can be sustained for the long haul.

Having a clear sense of meaning and purpose is a key area in being resilient. If you are crystal clear about your reasons for being alcohol-free, your sense of purpose will bust any temptation to drink. That's why I keep nagging you to do your purpose statement. If your purpose becomes stale, do a new one. Review it regularly to ensure it is relevant to your life now, and today.

Key practices to improve your sense of meaning and purpose:

- Refine your purpose in getting sober
- Update your purpose as your life moves on
- Ensure you are attending to your basic health needs to avoid feeling below par which can affect mood.

Problem-solving and dealing with stress.

Low (0 – 3)

Do you see life as one long problem? Does each day feel like a treadmill followed by an obstacle course? Do people just seem to come up with one problem after another? You might be the sort of person who feels this way. Your life just feels like one long series of difficult issues and challenges that vex you.

Perhaps you just keep your head down and your fingers crossed, avoiding problems as much as possible and keeping out of the line of fire. You do anything to keep the peace. Your life might feel overwhelming. Taking a drink feels like a welcome relief from all the hardship.

Perhaps faced with a challenge or confrontation, you feel compelled to fight back, defending your corner. This leaves you feeling even more stressed. Alternatively, you might just freeze, unable to respond, and then slink off feeling inadequate. You might be tempted to avoid dealing with problems, such as hiding bills or not responding to demands for repayments. Deal with problems as they arise. Most people will respond to a genuine request to make a plan for repayment over time.

If you are going to get alcohol-free, it is worth spending some time adopting a new approach to life's problems. You can ask for help. It is okay to get some support. It is acceptable to get family members, friends, work colleagues, or neighbors on board to help with practical tasks. It is not all up to you. If you think this, challenge that thought. If you have a long list of chores, write them all down and then talk to your spouse, child, housemate, or co-worker and decide who will do what. It is not all up to you. Take time out to relax and enjoy life. Rest is not a luxury; it is a human need. Learning about boundary setting will help give you the confidence to deal with challenges and confrontations in a healthy way.

Average (4 – 7)

On the whole, you roll with life's ups and downs. You might feel stressed at times, but you have strategies to deal with it. You might sometimes take on too much or get overenthusiastic about projects. Remember to take time out to just relax and enjoy yourself.

When faced with a challenge or confrontation you tend to take an assertive approach and deal with it head-on. You don't dwell unduly on past mistakes. You try to learn from them and move on. Generally, you are comfortable asking other people for help with practical tasks. You seek out support when you feel lonely or low. You accept that sometimes you can't solve a problem or it's not yours to solve. You can live with this and don't get hung up about it. Most days you feel upbeat and confident about dealing with problems.

High (8 – 10)

You enjoy a challenge and see it as an opportunity to learn more about yourself and the world. You approach problems as puzzles that need to be solved. You are not deterred if your first attempts at sorting out an issue are not immediately successful. You are happy to take on board a range of ideas and try them out. You tend to think creatively.

All this is great news, but remember to take on board how other people might be feeling in a difficult situation. Not everyone is as naturally upbeat as you. You might get frustrated by other people's perceived negativity. This frustration could catapult you quickly into a downward spiral towards a drink, so keep it all in balance. You don't have to agree with others but just accept how they feel, empathize if you can, and move on.

Finally, don't make life any harder than it needs to be. Life can certainly be full of challenges, but if you are having a period of plain sailing enjoy it while it lasts. You don't need to make problems for yourself to solve.

Key practices to improve how you solve problems and deal with stress:
- Ask for help
- Have a range of strategies to deal with stress
- Deal with issues as they arise. Accept that some problems are not within your control.

Do you think realistically about your life? Do you feel optimistic about it?

Low (0 – 3)

This question might pee you off. You think being realistic is acknowledging that life sucks and that's it. Optimism is for Pollyanna. You get annoyed with self-help books telling you it's all your fault. You can't remember the last time you felt even a glimmer of happiness. You might be really angry that you 'can't' drink anymore.

You get irritated by the 'toxic positivity' touted by health freaks, 'Insta-influencers' and self-help gurus.

And you know what? So, do I.

Life is not black and white. Bad things happen to good people and there are no easy answers. Forced cheerfulness, denying any difficult feelings, and running away from reality are not healthy. None of us can feel one hundred percent positive all of the time.

The opportunity to sit in a cesspool of anger, resentment and regret is open to everyone. No judgment. I say this with all compassion. Sit in the pool for a while. Experience it. Wallow for a bit if you want. But when it gets too boring, painful, or stinky, start to inch out. Just a bit.

To get you started on the journey out of the cesspool you can ponder on some big questions. Questions such as, 'What is deeply important to you?' *To you.* Not your parents, spouse, or family, but to *you.* 'What sort of person do you want to be?' 'If you were enjoying life, what would you be doing?'. These sorts of questions help us to work out our values. When we are clear about our values, we feel vitalized and experience life as rich and full even when it hurts.

Average (4 – 7)

On the whole, you feel upbeat about your life. You have off-days and you are aware of your issues, but you feel a sense of optimism about overcoming most difficulties. Sometimes you might be overly optimistic and wing it, expecting everything to turn out fine. For example, you might go on a car journey to a new town without taking a map or checking the route before you go. You get lost, the GPS takes you on a weird route and you get frustrated and anxious about being late for an appointment. You had been overly optimistic about finding your way around an unknown town. Perhaps you do this with drinking. You know it causes problems for you, but you are overly optimistic that the next time will be okay. Of course, it's not.

Alternatively, you might have days during which you feel low about life, especially about yourself. You might struggle to think of anything good about yourself or your life. Your mood sometimes dictates how you feel about life in general on any given day.

High (8 – 10)

You can accept good days and bad days without getting too over-excited or down. When assessing your abilities and areas to develop, you are fairly realistic and accept your limitations. But you do acknowledge your skills and talents.

When dealing with other people, you can accept them as they are without trying to fix them. Most days you feel upbeat about your life, even if challenges are going on. You deal with issues as they arise and plan as best you can, to avoid problems. You do not dwell unduly on past mistakes but learn from them and move on. You accept that life is a mixed bag of experiences. You keep your expectations in check and don't expect anyone or any situation to be perfect.

Key practices to improve thinking realistically about life:

- Accept that life and people are a mix of good and bad. Avoid black-and-white thinking.
- Don't expect too much of people or situations. But be open to surprises.
- Enjoy the present but spend some time thinking ahead and making plans as needed. Having a plan saves time, helps pre-empt problems, and gives you peace of mind.

Self-development and growth.

Low (0-3)

As far as you are concerned you did your learning at school and the day you left, you just wanted to get on with earning a living and enjoying life. Learning new stuff was boring.

You want to have a good time and feel good, fast. The drink helped you do that but now you find that you don't always get that good time, or you realize it is costing you too much. This is a dilemma. You need to find a new way to get through life. This means you need to learn new attitudes and skills.

You do not need to change your personality. You do not need to do weird stuff. You do not need to become a yogi, a guru, or a saint. But you can learn new things that make life easier and more enjoyable.

Remind yourself that everyone can learn new things. Think back to activities you have enjoyed and start small. Pick up a book or watch a video on your subject of interest and build on that.

Average (4 – 7)

You enjoy learning new stuff. You might struggle with self-confidence when taking on something new. Perhaps you question yourself a lot and worry you are not progressing as much as other people.

You might have set ideas about activities you are naturally good at and shy away from areas you feel you have no talent for. Remember it is helpful to your personal growth to try out new things, especially subjects or activities that you might have struggled with in the past. This puts you out of your comfort zone. When you do this, the fact that you have put yourself out there builds your self-confidence. Also, you might surprise yourself and find out you are skilled in an area you had dismissed before. For example, many of us might have been put off sports, science, or math because we had poor experiences at school. As an adult, when we go back to learn more about them, we find we are interested and can solve the math equation, hit the ball, or take on a scientific theory that baffled us years before. The effort of learning something new is good for the brain and our self-esteem.

High (8 -10)

You love learning new stuff. You get twitchy if you don't have a fresh challenge lined up. You enjoy thinking creatively and applying new concepts to your life. You see learning as a life-long journey.

Self-growth is your pet subject. You are always looking for ways to improve your life and hone your skills. If you are not actively engaged in a new course or learning a new skill you feel a bit lost.

You welcome novel ideas and are stimulated by being in the company of people who are similar to you. This thirst for knowledge and improving your skills gives you a great sense of personal purpose and meaning. You feel excited and motivated when starting a new course of study.

As in all things keep this in balance and don't take on too much. Also, remember it is okay to take time out to process new information and apply concepts to your life. Don't be in too much of a hurry to get onto the next new thing.

Key practices to improve learning and self-growth:

- Remember TREAT? The 'A 'stands for *Absorb uplifting content every day*. Every day read, listen to or learn something that helps you feel motivated to stay well and grow as a person.
- Pick out an area you loved to learn about as a child or when you were younger and start doing a bit of

research on books, courses, or videos to grow your learning in that area of interest.

- Push yourself out of your comfort zone and sign up for a new class. Take up a new hobby or sport and watch your resilience grow.

***

I have spent two chapters on resilience because it is such a key skill in riding the ups and downs of life. As it is a big topic, I have broken it down into five key areas.

Remember you do not have to tackle all the areas of resilience at once.

Look at your scores and focus on the area you need to develop most. Focus on this one area for a while. Pick just one key practice you can apply to your life and take that away with you today. Build it into your daily plan which I summarized as TREAT – the A standing for 'absorb uplifting content'. You don't need to do anything extra to grow your resilience. For example, if you want to improve how you handle stress, you can focus on reading or listening to material that gives you ideas on how to do that.

Your resilience will change over time, so redo this exercise regularly to work out which area you need to focus on.

Summary:
- Focus on one area of resilience you want to improve on based on your scores.
- Pick out one key practice and build that into your daily routine.

- When you feel stronger in that area, complete the Resilience Tracker exercise again and focus on a new area to improve on.

Playing the Game.

When do you play? Seriously, do you get out to play a sport or play cards? How often do you feel playful? Do you ever pull out your art and craft supplies to just mess about with them rather than create something useful? Do you abandon art projects if you feel they don't look right or meet specific aesthetic criteria?

You might be wondering what this has to do with getting sober or with the drinking culture. Don't laugh and don't get cross with me. I'm not just glibly recommending you find a hobby. I am specifically talking about playing and being playful. Play releases endorphins improve brain function and stimulate creativity. If you are ditching the booze or working to sustain sobriety, this is good news.

Our society is dismissive of play for adults, seeing it as a frivolous and irresponsible waste of time. For many adults, personal and professional responsibility pushes out opportunities to play. The only type of acceptable play for adults is a competitive sport, but specifically as a woman, do you have a chance to engage even in that?

Do you ever have time to daydream, or to enjoy the process of creating something without a fixed outcome of what it should look like? Do you ever doodle or try your hand at drafting a poem? In his book *'Play'* Stuart Brown, MD has studied the positive effect of play in our lives as adults and the consequences of no play, which include isolation, depression, criminal behavior, and physical disease.

There can seem to be an endless list of things that we need to do – serious things that need our attention and that only we can perform correctly. As workers with a home to look after and children to take care of, the very idea of playing seems ridiculous. It's much easier to just keep trundling along and pour ourselves another glass of wine to mask the fatigue, resentment, or feelings of overwhelm.

Sitting down with a glass of prosecco might be the only time you sit down. Ideas of relaxation and unwinding become enmeshed with drinking alcohol. As you throw yourself down onto the sofa at night after the dishes are washed, the schoolbags and lunch boxes are packed, the kitchen is cleaned, and you have done your final check of work emails and prepared your presentation for the following day – or not – that first sip of alcohol acts as a relaxing balm for all the stress and anxiety. It might be the only time you have sat down all day since your alarm woke you that morning.

What is play and what does it look like to you? Brown, the author of the book '*Play,*' calls it a "state of being, purposeless, fun and pleasurable''. The focus is on the joy of the experience. For Brown, who is in his eighties, it is playing tennis with his friends and walking his dog.

Take a moment now to recall what relaxation or having fun looks like for you. What picture instantly flashes into your mind? Does it involve a drink? What do you look forward to at the end of a busy day taking care of the kids or out working, or both? You might also have older relatives to take care of or extra duties on top of what you must do in your own home.

When do you get to play?

I remember the feeling of sheer exhaustion when my family was young and at home. It's hard working forty or fifty or more hours per week and then coming home to start cooking, cleaning, helping with the kids' homework, and organizing lunchboxes and physical education kits for school. As women with careers, studies, and families, we might be having it all, but we are doing it all too. When is there time to play? You laugh cynically and pour yourself another drink.

If you have been able to put down the booze, even that effort too can turn into another work project. That's not to say it is not serious – it could be life or death – but as the famous Irish writer Oscar Wilde said: "Life is too serious to be taken seriously." Some of the most creative and successful people in history have taken on a playful attitude to life, so don't dismiss it. Look at your attitude towards your sobriety or moderation of your drinking. In recovery circles, they talk about 'white-knuckling it' – hanging onto sobriety with a grim determination. Is this how sobriety is for you? How long will it last if it is just another arduous task on top of the challenging work that is in your life?

You might attend recovery meetings you hate because you feel you must. You might look at your calendar with a sigh and tick off another sober day, feeling deprived of the fun, spontaneity, or feelings of release you got from the booze. How long will this sobriety last?

It's a quirk of human nature that when we turn something into a game, it becomes more fun. Even the most tedious tasks take on a lighthearted challenge if we make them into a game. You might have used this approach to cajole your kids to clear up or tidy away toys: ''Who can get the most picked up? How many toys can you pack away by the time I count to ten? Who can get dressed first?'' Kids love a game – it's motivating and lightens the atmosphere. Getting a job done becomes playful and injects energy and enthusiasm. Adults are just big kids, and we enjoy a game too.

You will have heard the expression 'boys and their toys'. The men in our lives seem to find it much easier than women to pick up a game to play – games that take them out of the home and connects them with friends or others with the same interest. I am speaking in very general terms and there will be exceptions. Perhaps the man in your life is extremely focused on the home and family. If he is, that is a wonderful thing, and you will be able to get him on board to help you at home to be available for some self-care and play. This can be done individually and as a couple.

However, speaking from personal experience of friends, family acquaintances, and just looking around at our culture in the western world in the twenty-first century, I see women working hard to keep the home functioning and showing up in the workplace with drive, determination, and a perceived need to keep it all going. And that's it. That's their life.

This is not about bashing men or criticizing men. It is about making sure we show up for ourselves as women, treating ourselves and our lives respectfully. Without some joy, some lightness of spirit, life becomes one long grim to-do list. If your life feels like a treadmill, and that a gin and tonic, a glass of red wine, or Pimm's is the only bright light in your life, it's time to look at how we can lighten up and just play.

A question for you: When you think of golf, fishing, football, field sports, card games, or sailing, how many young or middle-aged women do you see enjoying them? Can you think of any mothers in your circle of friends who enjoy playing any sports or games? Do you take time out to participate in anything that gets you connected with other people, moves your body in a way that makes you feel good, and extends skills or personal attributes? I'm not talking about grimly working out to get toned or lose weight. I'm not talking about sewing or knitting because you must repair your child's school uniform or make a warm scarf for them. I'm talking about participating in an activity for its own sake.

Another question for you: When you think about golf, fishing, football, sports, or sailing, how many men do you know go off at weekends or days out with friends to enjoy these activities? I reiterate this is not about engendering resentment or anger against the men in our lives, I'm just asking the question. Based on anecdotal and personal experience it looks like lots of men find the time to enjoy playing as well as working and taking care of families. So, it's time for us ladies to create opportunities to play too.

I get it. You might be reading this and thinking, yeah, I hardly have enough energy to drag myself into work, get the kids organized, and put food on the table – and you're asking me to play too. But I am saying this with all kindness and compassion for your circumstances. Having these attitudes of resentment, anger and a sense of victimization gives you a green light to drink. 'Hey, if you had my life, you would drink too!' I agree, yes, if the circumstances of your life are grim, what's going on would drive any reasonable human being to drink. But who is going to change it?

The system stinks. We don't have adequate affordable childcare. Most women work double shifts: one at home and another at work. As women, we are expected to show up as workers (but don't ask for time off for the kids too often…) and as mothers (make sure you have baked cakes for the school sale, attend all the school performances and teacher meetings, and never be late picking your kids up). Oh, and look like a magazine model while doing it all – no pressure!

No wonder we pick up the wine, or the prosecco, or the gin. But before you collapse into a gin-induced heap of self-pity, let me just say that we might be in a broken system, but we can take responsibility for ourselves. By carrying on as we are – work, clean, shop, care for the kids, drink, and repeat – we are contributing to the continuation of that pattern.

So, buck the trend by having the audacity to put your hand up and say: hey I'd like to enjoy my life too.

Your life is worth more than living like a robot, using 'mommy juice' to fuel the actions of the automaton you may feel you have turned into. Your life is worth more than a drink-saturated *half-life*.

You might feel like you will need to make some radical changes to your lifestyle to make this happen. First, you need to work out what you want to do (more on this later). Next, you need to get your partner and family on board. If they see that you have been struggling with the booze or it has become a major problem in your life, most loving partners will do what they can to make it happen. But some won't. Some might dig their heels in to maintain the status quo. Some might miss the sense of control or power they have over you as the drunken or even just slightly tipsy, ineffectual, struggling human being who is their wife or partner. So be prepared for backlash. Some partners might even be slightly disapproving or critical of your efforts to cut out the booze, as they might feel threatened. Some partners will be indifferent and continue to drink themselves – seeing it as your problem.

But keep the focus on you. What do you want to do? How do you want to play? What appeals to you? Next, work out how you can get to do it. This might be hard. You will need to make substantial changes at work and home. Cut back on hours, change the household budget to accommodate this, ask for help, and pay for help, but don't lose sight of how important it is to your recovery.

'Yeah right ', you might be thinking. 'I can't afford to cut my hours.'But, look at it this way if you drink in a way that has caused you problems your job might be at risk anyway. Working fewer hours has been proven to increase productivity, so cutting your hours will make you more productive, and happier and aid your recovery.

If you are still not convinced about the importance of play and of making life worth living by creating opportunities to enjoy it, let me share with you an observation based on real-life, full-on recovery treatment.

Some years ago, I worked in a private, specialist unit for people with addiction issues. We worked with a range of people who were addicted to prescription medication, over-the-counter sleeping aids, and a range of other drugs, but the most common issue was alcohol dependence. If you had visited the unit without prior knowledge of its purpose, you might easily have mistaken it for a high-end, plush hotel. There were fresh cut flowers on the reception desk, the carpets were deep and soft, and the furnishings were tasteful and of excellent quality. There was a gym, a craft room, a games room, and a 9-hole golf course. The grounds were extensive and well-maintained. Residents were encouraged to use all the facilities. They were frequently out strolling, jogging, cycling around the grounds, or playing on the golf course. Staff wore normal clothes rather than uniforms and took on the role of supportive friends. We were instructed to facilitate choices to enhance the residents' enjoyment and relaxation. Some residents booked themselves in as a once-a-year treat to maintain or re-establish sobriety.

The services of such an establishment might be beyond your needs, desires, or budget, but you can emulate some of the principles of the care offered. There were regular recovery meetings. The staff members were cheerful and upbeat, encouraging residents to take part in activities they enjoyed or develop interests in new sports, games, or hobbies. There were sessions on nutrition, exercise advice, regular yoga, meditation, and relaxation classes.

This well-respected institution saw the benefits of play – of hobbies, interests, sports, and games – as part of a recovery package. So, give yourself the optimum chances of a successful recovery at home by building enjoyable activities into your routine. This will not just help you get well, but to stay well in the long term. If you feel that playing is frivolous, re-frame it as an essential component of your recovery package. It's not an optional extra.

In 1978 a psychologist named Bruce Alexander conducted some ground-breaking research, the outcomes of which changed how addiction was perceived by the medical world and professionals working in the field. You might have heard of the experiment. Johan Hari talked about it in a TED talk that went viral. Bruce Alexander wanted to prove that a person's mental, emotional, and psychological state was the greatest cause of addiction and not the drug itself.

In research environments, rats are usually kept in small, cramped spaces and housed alone. In Alexander's experiment, he housed the rats in large cages, two hundred times the size of the usual cages, and put them together in mixed groups, free to run around and do what rats like to do. Like most humans, rats are sociable, industrious creatures who thrive on having things to do and ratty friends to do them with. Put rats in solitary and like humans, they don't fare so well. Alexander built a 'rat park.' There were wheels, bells, equipment to scurry round on and in, lots of space, all the food they needed, and two sources of liquid.

One source of liquid was plain water, and the other was a morphine solution. The rats in the rat park preferred the plain water. In contrast, the solitary rats kept in tiny cages with the same choice of drinks drank nineteen times more of the morphine solution. In addition, the rats who were previously alone and addicted to the morphine appeared to ignore the morphine solution when placed in the rat park, voluntarily suffering withdrawal while they scurried about playing on the rat wheels and socializing with their furry friends. The research team concluded that drug dependence was not caused by the drug but was a result of being isolated and bored.

The findings of the Rat Park experiment were not popular because they contradicted much of the understanding of addiction at the time. When it has been talked about since, such as in Hari's TED talk, it has created a lot of excitement. I am not saying this is the whole story. I am certainly not over-simplifying addiction. The Rat Park approach does not address issues of deep trauma that may have changed the brains of the child or young person affected to such a degree that they become hard-wired for addiction. Today, psychologists acknowledge that addiction involves transmitters in the brain that alters the way users feel and think. Scientists now realize that addiction is as much mental as it is physical. Having enjoyable, engaging activities and a sense that life is worth living must, at the very least, optimize the chances of a successful recovery.

The other criticism of the Rat Park experiment outcomes is that real life for human beings is no rat park. People have stress, pressures, deadlines, chores, jobs, and responsibilities. For many of us, the hustle culture is the air we breathe. But we do have choices. We can choose to be part of it and dumb down our natural feelings of exhaustion, loneliness, and overwhelm with alcohol. Or we can decide that our lives are worth living and make some changes to make space for things we love to do – experiences that make us feel alive, vibrant, and cheerful.

Not everyone wants to or can afford to do lots of yoga classes, attend spas or meditate. You might even feel nauseous at the prospect of these sorts of activities. I am not suggesting that you float around on an Instagram cloud of calm perfection. Real life will go on. That is even more reason to build in what you love to do, whether it's kayaking, camping, netball, or backgammon. Do what you enjoy and do it regularly.

Feeling part of the pack is another significant finding from Rat Park: we need to feel like we belong. So, all the better if you engage in activities that involve being with others.

If you are still resistant to the idea of adopting a more playful approach to your life and recovery, sit with this resistance. Experience it and be curious about why that might be. Is it hard to let go of feeling like a victim? This might be why you drink. So, if you are not a victim, you don't need to drink, and this is where the resistance comes from: you don't want to stop drinking.

But I guess you are reading this because you do want to stop or have stopped and want to maintain recovery or are worried about picking up again. Or you don't want to let go of demanding work because if you let go of being busy, needed, or ambitious, what remains? You could be addicted to work to numb the feelings and then you drink to numb the feelings some more. Do you brandish workaholic tendencies as a badge of honor and your importance in the world? Just why are you so busy anyway? What's it all about? Just how important is it? I ask these questions with all compassion and understanding to help you drill down to what is stopping you from letting go of behaviors that might be sabotaging your recovery.

If you are not ready to stop drinking or are not ready to let go of the compulsion to be constantly busy, be gentle with yourself. Don't force anything. You are already beaten up by ideas of what you should be, or ought to be, or how you should show up in the world. Be kind to yourself. Give it some time. If it feels like too much to have a hard conversation with your partner about pulling their weight at home or helping with the kids, just tell them how you feel without a grand plan outlining your desired activities. Start the dialogue, express your emotions and be open to the outcomes. Perhaps your spouse or co-parent of your children did not realize how much you were struggling, so let them know.

If you lost contact with yourself and don't know what you would enjoy, think back to when you were a child or young person. Were you on a swimming team? Did you play hockey or go ice skating? Did you love camping and orienteering with the Girl Guides or a scout group?

If thinking back to your childhood is difficult or you can only remember deprivations or had to shoulder responsibility too young, connect with the playful part of you. In her book *'The Artists Way,'* Julia Cameron suggests taking yourself out on a date. Go to an art gallery, collect shells on the beach, go to a theatre or go out to do something that you think will be fun. She also suggests writing 'morning pages' – spend a few minutes first thing in the morning writing without censoring what you write – a type of stream of consciousness or 'brain dump' to unload what is on your mind. This process could help shift what might be hindering your efforts to let go of overworking and feeling miserable.

Finally, if you are so wedded to the idea of being productive and your work ethic is binding you in a stranglehold that is squeezing the joy out of life, here are a few additional tips to get you started:

Change your attitude towards the concept of play. See it as a necessary component of being more creative, thinking more clearly, being more productive, and sustaining your recovery from alcohol dependence. Play can just be about being more playful in your day-to-day activities. You can incorporate a more playful attitude into mundane or ho-hum tasks. My son used to groan with a smile, rolling his eyes skywards, shaking his head in mock ruefulness, when I danced to music in the supermarket as we pushed a trolley of shopping around. You could playfully slap your partner on the bottom in public, tickle their toes, or ruffle their hair – just be playful. Read aloud to your kids or partner and act out the stories or the prose.

Lay it on thick. For adults, writers such as Frank McCourt or Dylan Thomas are meant to be read aloud -playfully.

Connect with friends who are playful and take life and themselves lightly. Share silly videos, jokes, and anything that makes you feel happier or more cheerful. Engage with your children in their play, not just *watch* them play. Build dens, sit under the table, pretend you are a bear in a cave, go on adventures, and build sandcastles. If you have young children in your life, fully immerse yourself in the play experience. You will be helping yourself and doing more for them in terms of encouraging their creativity and being a fantastic role model. Much more than the latest gadget or after-school program could ever do.

As Brown says in his book '*Play*': ''Play is the purest expression of love.'' So, show yourself, your family, friends, and the world some love. Play.

Summary:

- Play is essential to sound emotional, mental, and physical health. High-end recovery facilities recognize this and encourage clients to develop interests to aid recovery from alcohol dependence. You can do this at home for yourself.
- Games, sports, crafts, and hobbies all come under the banner of 'play'.
- If you struggle to find time to play, try changing your attitude to be more playful and fun. Look for opportunities to turn everyday activities and tasks into a game.

Feeling Comfortable in Your Skin.

Perhaps you have always felt like you have a layer of protective skin missing. Maybe when you were a child, people told you that you were too sensitive. Do you chide yourself for overreacting when you feel someone has left you out or not noticed how hard you are working? Do you get irritated easily? Do you feel like everyone is getting at you and find it hard not to take things personally? Does feeling comfortable in your skin sound like a pipedream?

Perhaps you drank to ease some of these uncomfortable feelings. Maybe you don't remember, but now that you have cut down or stopped drinking, all these intense, overwhelming emotions hit you.

The early days of stopping drinking can feel like a crazy time. One day you can feel like the world is full of sparkling rainbows, dancing unicorns, and sunshine. The next day you might feel like you have been thrown into a dark pit of despair.

So, you will need to put some effort into achieving some emotional balance. But what does that mean and how do you achieve it?

Emotional balance means you feel comfortable in your skin, feeling fairly relaxed most of the time. You can see a situation from someone else's point of view and don't take every comment or remark to heart. You can take on board constructive criticism and make improvements if needed, or shrug it off if you feel the criticism is unwarranted. You enjoy life most of the time. Events that used to rock you off balance just seem to bounce off you.

When we take care of our emotional health, we handle the ups and downs of life. All human beings need to attend to their emotional well-being. Alcohol messes with our emotional health. Being sober is the first step in establishing a foundation for emotional balance. Working on emotional balance in the context of sobriety is called emotional sobriety.

Emotional sobriety is different from physical sobriety. Ideally, it is the state that goes along with being free from the effects of alcohol on the body. Being sober is more than just being dry. It means you respond to people in a kind and positive way. You don't take everything personally. You deal with other people in a calm and measured way. You might feel a flash of anger or irritation, but you can let it go. You don't hang on to resentments.

The following story illustrates what is *not* emotional sobriety. Miranda generously shared this in the early days of her sobriety.

Miranda was struggling to maintain her short period of sobriety and felt raw. Without the anesthetic of alcohol, she felt like an extra layer of skin had been peeled off, and all her senses and emotions were extra-sensitive. She recalled how she had a particularly tough day at work when everything seemed to go wrong. She felt completely inadequate and was convinced she was going to lose her job. Miranda was attending AA and had a sponsor, Kath. Miranda was concerned about the intensity of her difficult feelings, so she decided to visit Kath straight after work.

Miranda arrived on her sponsor's doorstep and rang the doorbell nervously. Kath opened the door, the phone to her ear. Kath smiled and indicated for Miranda to come in. As Miranda followed Kath down the hallway, she caught snippets of the phone conversation. She heard Kath say with a laugh, ''….no, not my *friend*! Okay, yes, I'll go now…bye, bye…''. Miranda felt a thud in her chest and could hardly breathe. Kath was talking about *her*.

Miranda had thought they were friends. She felt devastated, she burst into floods of tears as Kath stood perplexed, the smile gone from her face, replaced by concern and sympathy.

When Miranda composed herself, she said what she had heard Kath just say on the phone and the effect it had on her. Kath listened and smiled. Kath then went on to explain that she had been talking about a new boyfriend who she referred to as her '*friend*' in a joking way when talking to her sister. She hadn't been talking about Miranda at all.

As they discussed Miranda's intense emotions about feeling not accepted as a friend, Miranda realized how much she feared being rejected and how familiar this type of scenario was for her.

In this example, Miranda picked up on the words in a conversation that was nothing to do with her. She took it personally and overreacted. A lack of emotional sobriety means that often we over-react in this way. We will take innocent comments to heart and react in a way that is all out of proportion to what has happened.

Much later in her sobriety journey, Miranda shared the following story with me to illustrate her growth in her emotional sobriety:

After one year of being sober, Miranda felt strong enough to start dating again. She had worked through many of her issues with rejection, but she felt nervous about being hurt. Kath reminded her that her efforts in recovery were a 'bridge to normal living' and it was time to get on with her life and take a few risks.

Miranda had started to date Scott, an easygoing mechanic who she'd met when she had car trouble. Scott had arranged to meet Miranda for a walk along the seafront in their town and an early dinner. That afternoon he had phoned her at work and explained that he wouldn't be able to make it as he had a fleet of cars to sort at the garage. He reckoned he just wouldn't be finished and cleaned up in time for their date and he needed to cancel. Miranda understood and instead got a takeaway and went to a meeting that night.

When she woke up the next morning and replied to a cheery text from Scott, it dawned on her that she just accepted he was working and didn't feel at all upset. For Miranda, this was major progress and an encouraging sign of her growing emotional sobriety.

We never arrive at a point of complete emotional sobriety, but we will see markers of progress, just like Miranda spotted in herself.

Of course, people who are not in recovery and not addicted to a substance or behavior can take things personally and act out – 'punishing' people for letting them down with sour silences and holding a grudge. They can take offense in situations where none was intended and be in constant conflict with others. We probably all know people like that.

Emotional sobriety could also be referred to as 'maturity' or 'wisdom' and that is what all evolving, growing human beings need to work towards. It is a constant work in progress and not just limited to people with substance misuse issues. However, often the substance issues will highlight the need for emotional sobriety. Many people in recovery will be aware of the need for emotional sobriety, or wisdom or maturity, in a way that people without these issues may not be aware of.

But does emotional sobriety help keep you sober? Read Jill's story and you decide:

Jill had stopped drinking about three months previously as she felt it was damaging her relationship with her husband. He had suggested she go to AA, but Jill insisted she was okay and could handle it on her own. She just needed to stop drinking. It would be easy. She had stopped before for months at a time. She could do it again.

The evenings were the hardest part of the day for Jill. She had been a regular night-time drinker and missed her bottle of wine. She had sighed and fretted each evening, not able to settle to read or watch TV. She had taken to doing housework in the evenings, banging resentfully through the house with a vacuum.

Phil, her husband, agreed not to drink anymore at home, but he liked to snack in the evenings and watch TV. She was sure her husband deliberately got in the way when she was trying to clean. Just when she decided to clean the shower, he would disappear into the bathroom, and she would have to bang on the door to get him out. She was sure he munched on messy snacks just to wind her up, dropping crumbs where she had cleaned up. Jill complained and sighed. Eventually, her husband started to go out with his local running club in the evenings.

One Friday night she cracked. Instead of cleaning, she went to the local convenience store and bought not one but two bottles of her favorite wine.

"He made me do this." she sobbed into her glass. "He's left me on my own after all I've done for him."

You can see clearly how Gill's thinking and behavior – definitely not emotionally sober – led her right back to a drink. So, working on emotional sobriety will help you stick to an alcohol-free life. Not only will it help you to stay chemically sober, but you will feel better in your skin. You will feel more comfortable and at peace.

In addition, spending time alone will be precious solitude and not an angst-ridden experience to run away from. Emotional sobriety has many benefits, so it is well worth the effort.

So, just how do you work towards emotional sobriety? If you are newly sober, you might be feeling a hot mess of tangled emotions, resentments, and fears. How do you even begin to work on unpicking all this?

Perhaps, you have had repeated attempts at long-term sobriety but after a while, something happens, you overreact and like Gill in the example above, you go back to the bottle in a state of rage, hurt or crushing disappointment. Working on emotional sobriety will help you stay sober for the long haul.

Many of the subjects covered in this book will help you achieve and maintain a level of emotional sobriety. The following is a summary of what to focus on:

- Self-awareness
- Self-compassion
- Letting go of shame
- Changing beliefs
- Letting go of grudges – forgiving ourselves and others.
- Establishing boundaries

Women also have certain times of life or the month that will present extra challenges to emotional sobriety. Sometimes we feel insecure, overly sensitive, take things personally, get easily wound up, and are overly critical of others and especially ourselves. We dissolve into floods of tears for no apparent reason. Sound familiar?

As a woman with hormonal ups and downs across the month and a lifetime of menses, pregnancies, and 'the change', these sorts of feelings can be very real. This extra hormonal challenge can unravel our efforts to stay sober.

How do you handle these additional hurdles to achieve a serene approach to life?

If you are anything like me, there have been times in my life or the month when I have wanted to have a full-on tantrum like a two-year-old – complete with stamping feet, a red face, and a few screams. However, I know I would: A. lose friends B. lose my job C. frighten my husband and family. And D. quite possibly, I would get carted off somewhere by people in white coats. So, what do we do when we want to lash out angrily or cry due to out-of-whack hormones?

First off, keep track of your cycle. Note dates in a diary or on your phone calendar. There are apps nowadays to help you keep track too. This can help you find a biological explanation for how you are feeling. You will still feel more wound up or sensitive than usual, but at least you know why. You can give your partner a heads up too. If they know it is a difficult time for you, there is more of a chance of them understanding what is going on and not taking your behavior to heart themselves. This can ease possible tension in close relationships and avoid unnecessary conflict or misunderstandings.

Perhaps you are irregular or are going through perimenopause, not quite sure of what is going on with your cycle. Perimenopause is the time leading up to menopause. It starts earlier than you might think. Symptoms such as an irregular cycle, night sweats, hot flashes, mood swings, depression, and anxiety are common. So even if you think you are too young, get a hormone level check done at the medical center.

Perimenopause often starts sneakily, with a few little changes or symptoms here and there, so you might not even realize it has started but it could be dramatically affecting how you feel.

So even if you find it difficult to keep track of your cycle, tune into how you are feeling physically. When it is that time of the month, tell-tale sensations will probably indicate a few days of more turbulent emotions ahead, such as tummy twinges or backache. In perimenopause, symptoms such as night sweats or hot flashes (or flushes, depending on which side of the Atlantic you live on) might get worse during menstruation.

Read the signs your body is telling you and give yourself a bit of slack. Take a sickie if you need it. Get a massage, take warm baths, and do nice things for yourself. Lower your standards and catch up when you feel better. Avoid certain people if you know they are going to push your buttons. Guard your emotional sobriety. Losing it might mean you pick up a drink or press the 'sod-it' button and buy yourself a bottle of wine or gin and end up feeling worse.

Even if the only constructive thing you have done during this difficult time is not to drink alcohol, you are doing well. Remind yourself of this.

Accept the feelings for what they are: the effects of raging, fluctuating hormones. You don't need to get a divorce or move countries – you just need to give yourself a break. If you feel the urge to cry without knowing why you don't need to start psychoanalyzing what is going on with you.

If the date or physical evidence indicates that something hormonal is going on, go with that and soothe yourself as best you can in your circumstances. Have a chat with an understanding friend. Get as physically comfy as possible.

Of course, if feelings of low mood, depression, or uncontrollable crying go on for longer than a few days, reach out to your doctor and get additional help if needed.

Often, the effects of these hormonal fluctuations can feel like a cloud passing over. Once it passed, the sun comes out and life returns to normality without the need for any drama. But if deeper psychological issues are going on with you, you will need extra support.

And before I close this chapter, just a reminder that even if you feel like an emotional tornado has hit you, it *will be okay.* It will pass. While it is raging, all you need to do is control what comes out of your mouth. Your feelings are your feelings. There is no shame in them. But how will you feel if you snap, snarl, or generally fly off the handle with every unfortunate individual who gets in your way?

So, a little restraint will help you feel better in the long term. Take a break. B-R-E-A-T-H-E and smile. You can explain calmly how you feel, this is not about repressing or dishonoring your feelings, but you don't need to go into attack mode and then get all wound up about it. It's okay to feel how you feel.

Ultimately, it is your words and behavior that affect others and bounce back on you, so take a moment to respond mindfully to situations and avoid 'shooting from the hip.'

Other chapters in this book cover the building blocks of achieving emotional sobriety, such as how to be kinder towards yourself, how to be more self-aware, dealing with shame, forgiveness, and boundary setting. These building blocks will help build and maintain solid emotional sobriety. This solid foundation will not only help keep you sober but help you feel comfortable in your skin so that you and all the people in your world can enjoy the benefits of your sobriety.

In the next two chapters, there are lots more ideas on how to deal with difficult feelings.

Summary:
- Early sobriety is an emotionally turbulent time.
- Emotional sobriety ideally accompanies physical sobriety. It means feeling emotionally stable, calm, and seeing things in perspective.
- Everyone can benefit from working on their emotional balance.

The Moodometer.

In the last chapter, I talked about how to achieve emotional balance. A key aspect of doing that is being aware of feelings and moods as they arise. This awareness can help you take prompt action before the mood takes hold and you find yourself reaching for a drink.

In the next chapter, *Busting a Bad Mood*, there are lots of practical tips to deal with difficult, passing feelings. In this chapter, I will focus on spotting the feeling before it gets out of control.

A meter is a device that helps us keep track of something. For example, I have a meter at home that tells me how much electricity I have used. This is useful and helps avoid unnecessary shocks when the bill arrives. In the same way, a Moodometer helps keep track of feelings by tuning into what is going on in your body and mind and responding to it before the shock of a full-on tantrum. You can take some small actions to feel calmer or more comfortable promptly.

So, the Moodometer is a useful approach for both keeping track of feelings and achieving a better mood when your emotional state has taken a nose-dive. When you are more attuned to small changes in your mood, you can notch up to a more pleasant mood with less drama.

Just before I explain how the Moodometer works, consider this: Feeling just okay doesn't necessarily mean you are depressed or low, *it's just okay*. Being just okay sometimes is ... well ... okay. Settle into the feeling with a spirit of comfortable contentment. If life were an exciting, one hundred percent exhilarating high all the time, it would wear us out. Also, when you are on a high, the only way is down.

Therefore, having a steady, contented sort of feeling is more sustainable and gives room to improve a little, without all the drama. So if you feel a tiny bit flat, see it as progress in how you are experiencing your emotions – fewer highs and devastating lows. What might initially feel like a gray mood will gradually take on interesting hues and more vibrant colors. You will start to feel a range of gentler emotions, such as contentment, satisfaction, pleasure, and simple enjoyment. A steady, cheerful disposition will become a default setting for you rather than the swings of emotion from high to low you might have got hooked on. It's not only external chemicals like alcohol we become addicted to. Many of us also get hooked on the adrenalin rush that accompanies intense mood swings and drama.

So that being said, let's get back to the Moodometer. This is how it works: Imagine a vertical meter or scale numbered from 0 up to 10. This Moodometer measures your mood. For example, 0 is the pits: a depressed, angry beyond words, grief-stricken, worried out-of-your-mind type feeling. 10 is intense joy: a mountain-top exhilaration, fit to burst with happiness sort of emotion.

The numbers in between are all the range of emotions in the middle, moving up from a bit low, to neutral, okay, contented, satisfied, cheerful, happy, and so on.

This mental picture of a scale that moves up and down is a visual sliding scale. And having our scale calibrated into 10 divisions helps ingrain the idea that we are gently notching up one or two. Thinking this way helps to move away from the habit of ricocheting dramatically from deep dips to surging highs with not much in between.

If you have become used to experiencing any slight downturn of mood with a negative reaction, you will begin to respond less fearfully. It's just a minor notch down, no big deal. You can respond with a small action to help you feel better. Even something as simple as a glass of water or a phone call with a friend can be enough to ease back up a little.

By taking care of your moods, you are less likely to get into the danger zone of extreme fatigue, isolation, hunger, thirst, or intense emotional pain that could lead you towards a bottle. Many women push themselves on and on into exhaustion, then when they feel lousy, a drink seems like a particularly tempting idea. The Moodometer helps avoid getting into the red-light zone of extremely uncomfortable feelings. You will relearn how to respond to a small dip in the mood without drama – especially drama that could involve taking a drink when you don't want to.

So, the Moodometer can help upgrade feelings in a more calibrated way from bad, to better, to good. So, for example, you wake up and feel lousy. You shuffle to the bathroom and groan at your reflection. The kitchen is messy, it's raining outside, and you remember you are seeing a particularly difficult client that day at work. You get the picture.

No matter how hard you try, you are not going to snap out of the Monday morning blues and jump on your pink unicorn and fly off into a sparkly rainbow. It just isn't going to happen no matter how many positive affirmations you make or how long your gratitude list is. So instead of falsely trying to force yourself from a low score of 1 up to a 10, do something simple that will help you creep up from a 1 to a 3, such as taking a shower.

Okay so now you are at a 3. Have breakfast, your blood sugar goes up a little, and you feel a bit more human. Put on some upbeat music, get dressed, spray on your favorite perfume and now you're at a 4. You are not feeling like you have won the lottery, but at least you are feeling more comfortable as you go out the door and get on with your day.

So, concentrate your efforts on moving up gradually. Keep doing those next right things to keep moving up. You might go down again as you battle through heavy traffic, so put on a positive audiobook and feel buoyed up a little.

The Moodometer can also be used to cope with a sudden, dramatic downturn in mood, especially flashes of anger. For example, consider this scenario: You've had a great trip out. You've been cycling with friends on a summer evening, there has been an awesome sunset, great banter, lots of laughs, and you feel exhilarated from the exercise.

You get home in a high mood, chuckling to yourself as you think about a joke your friend shared with you. Still smiling, you skip into the living room. You stop dead in your tracks.

There are toys on the floor, the remnants of a takeaway meal on the coffee table and your one-year-old is running around with a full diaper. Your partner looks up sourly from their laptop and you feel your stomach sink. "You're late," he says. How would you be feeling now?

Are you plummeting from high up on the Moodometer to crashing at the bottom? This type of situation happens all the time. You have a nano-second to make a choice. If you explode in anger, how will it end? I don't need to paint a picture of the outcome. You might lift a drink on the back of it.

So how can the Moodometer help?

First, off register, how you feel, avoiding drama – disappointed, irritated? Perhaps you do feel volcano-like anger. That's okay, but keep a mental picture in mind of your Moodometer. This can help avoid a complete meltdown at that moment. See your Moodometer pinging at a bright red 0 and note it.

These few seconds of internal focus will give you space to take a breath, pause, and respond more calmly. You can then find the control to greet your child and suggest to your partner that you tidy up together. You don't need to go all Mary Poppins, but you can be civil. You can still *feel* anger – nothing wrong with that. But by *responding* calmly, you avoid heaping on a double whammy of regret about scary-angry behavior. By remaining calm, the outcome has a better chance of being a positive one.

Later, you can talk to your partner about the importance of changing the baby regularly and keeping a pleasant home environment for you all. But in the meantime, the room gets tidied, the baby gets changed and life goes on without the drama of a big row. The Moodometer has helped you slow down that torrent of emotion. It can act as a sort of gentle brake.

In the next chapter, we will look at various methods to shake off a bad mood, so keep reading.

Summary:

- A meter is a device to keep track of something.
- The Moodometer can help you keep track of small changes in mood. You can use this awareness to gently notch up to feeling more comfortable.
- This awareness helps avoid experiencing overwhelming feelings or moods. The type of feeling that could lead to a drink or behavior you later regret.

Busting a Bad Mood.

In the previous chapter, we looked in detail at the Moodometer. The Moodometer can be used as a tool to be more aware of emotions as they build up before they take hold. It can also be used to 'notch up' a mood from a low one to a more comfortable feeling. But what sorts of things can you do to improve your mood? How can you notch up from feeling like your dog has just died to a more comfortable state?

Note I used the term 'notch up'. Try to let go of the expectation that you will shoot up from a miserable 0 to a rapturous 10 in a few seconds. Aim to gently improve your mood and keep notching up until you feel happier, but it might take some time.

This chapter is full of techniques to help you feel happier and more content. Moods might come and go, but when you get stuck in the middle of the funk, it can be difficult to get out. And for many, that's a big trigger to drink. So, learning how to improve how you feel using alcohol-free methods is important for your sobriety.

You might have been told to just 'sit with the feeling'. It's all very well to sit with it, but what do you do when you feel like stamping on the floor and screaming like a two-year-old? If, you feel like a grumpy tiger, how do you restrain yourself from ripping someone to shreds, while still validating how you feel?

A reminder here is to practice tuning into a quiet, centered place inside yourself regularly. This does not have to be a full-on meditation practice, just a few minutes of calm. Don't wait until you are in a bad mood. Do it every day, no matter what mood you are in.

If this doesn't make sense, let's do it together, now. Just sit where you are. If possible, have your feet on the floor. Get comfortable. Stand up if you wish. Read through the next paragraph a couple of times if needed. When you can recall the basic ideas in the paragraph, close your eyes or look down, not focusing on anything and do what I suggest. You won't look weird. You will just look like you are thinking deeply about your book. So try it. Ready?

Okay. Breathe right the way down into your belly as slowly as you can. Let your shoulders drop. Focus on uplifting words such as energy, calm, peace, tranquility – whatever word or concept appeals to you. Feel your body relax as you breathe as slowly and deeply as you can. Have a sense of what is going on in your body. Breathe into it. Breathe out anything you feel is negative for you, such as fatigue, anger, frustration, or sadness. Keep doing this for a few minutes. Open your eyes.

That's it. Pretty simple. But I promise you, if you do it, your moods will improve. But you need to *do* it – just reading about it changes nothing.

Do this regularly. You can do this in most places. Just keep your eyes open if you are driving! Over time, when you do this in a neutral or good mood, you will connect with your default emotional setting, which is to be calm and content.

But how do you deal with that constant, repetitive, negative voice going around in your head? That voice that is telling you how awful your life is / how unreasonable another person has been / how infuriating your boss is / how difficult your child is / how it is not your fault / how hurt you feel / how sad you are. The voice that, no matter how Zen-like you try to be, won't just shut up. It goes on and on, causing you to grit your teeth in anger, bring tears to your eyes, or feel like someone is going at your belly with their fists.

You try to ignore it and get on with your work, watching a movie, reading a book, or having a conversation. But the voice drones on, bringing your mood down further. You can't concentrate or focus on anything else. It's like a broken record or a scratched CD. How the hell do you get rid of that?

This is what you do: pretend it is a radio in the background. You are not fighting it, arguing with it, or agreeing with it. It's just there like a background hum. You get on with what you are doing and allow the voice to rumble on in the background. As you take your focus off it, although it is still there on the edge, it will recede in your consciousness.

Have you ever been in a room with an annoying fluorescent tube that hums? As you sit in the room in silence, you become aware of it, and it seems to be getting louder. The more you focus on it, the louder it seems. Then there is a distraction, people come into the room, a conversation starts – and after a few minutes, you have forgotten about the irritating hum. It's still there but because you are not focused on it, it fades into the background.

If you are experiencing 'the voice' when you are alone with your thoughts and with no distractions, it can be hard to focus on something else. But try this: find a few words you can say over and over, like a mantra. They do not have to be particularly positive or insightful. They can be anything, as anything is better than arguing with the internal voice. Perhaps you have a positive affirmation or a word such as 'calm' or 'peace.' If you are spiritually inclined a short prayer or piece of scripture will work. Keep saying the words to yourself.

Concentrating on the words will break the repetitive train of thoughts going around and around in your head bringing your mood down. You are not ignoring it. You are aware of it, but you are deciding to focus your attention elsewhere.

Another variation of this method is to pick a large number – say 500 – and count backward. If you are quick with math and find this easy, you could count back from 500 in steps of 3 or 6.

Try reciting a poem from memory or lines learned from a play. Something that engages your brain and removes the focus away from negative, angry, or sad thoughts you've got stuck with. Eventually, that voice will quieten down and leave you in peace.

Perhaps you have been rattled by jaw-dropping bad service, a vicious online slur, or someone's outrageous behavior? Perhaps the bottom has dropped out of your world, and you are reeling from some bad news.

You might well have heard the expression: 'Letting someone live rent-free in your head.' Perhaps you are angry with someone or feel resentful about how they have treated you. You have arguments with them, but just in your head.

You recite to yourself what they have done or said or how they have behaved that has been so hurtful or outrageous. This could even be years or decades after the event.

This obsessive focus on someone else's behavior is giving that person space in your head. By focusing on something else like your mantra, prayer, calming word, or counting, you are in effect cutting off the power supply to the rent-free tenant. It's like forcing out a squatter by shutting off the electricity and water.

Sometimes we know why we are in a bad mood, at least on the surface. But sometimes a bad mood can seem to descend for no reason. It could be an internal trigger, of which you are not even consciously aware. You might realize why at a later point, or you might not.

Sometimes you just need to find a way to make the mood easier to deal with as it moves through you. The following are some techniques that are reminders for you. They are a bit of a first-aid list for a bad mood. I have listed those that are free or cheap, accessible in most situations, you can do in public without looking too weird, and do not need any special kit or equipment:

Breathe – slowly, deeply, and rhythmically. Research has proven time and time again that this will help. It's free and easy and you can do it anywhere, so try it. Don't dismiss it because it is free and simple.

Movement – a brisk walk, even just standing up tall and taking a few breaths will help. Stretching – that includes your face – stretch your mouth and smile. It's been proven to lift a sour mood.

Music – whatever does it for you. Queen's *'Don't Stop Me Now'* does it for me. If you can dance to it with all the cheesy moves, all the better.

Be thankful for the good stuff. Don't groan. Just try it. Pick out a few things you can see that you like – a tree, a flower, a chocolate muffin, whatever. If it makes you feel good, focus on it for a few seconds. If you don't feel grateful, don't force it. There's nothing wrong or bad about you if you don't feel a rush of gratitude, so don't heap on any more blame, just try something else.

Humor – Watch a funny video clip. The UK actor and comedian, Dawn French falling, waist-deep into a puddle in the British comedy show, 'The Vicar of Dibley' makes me giggle every time. I cannot stay grumpy when I watch that clip on YouTube. Look it up. I hope it makes you smile.

Play – Remember I talked about the benefits of play in the chapter *'Playing the Game'*? So, play with your dog, your child, or someone else's child (ask their parents first), or play a game, a sport, or a musical instrument.

Make tea – where I come from this is the solution to every ill. It might not solve every problem, but it makes it feel more bearable. So be comforted by the process of brewing up and drinking a nice, warm cup of tea.

Go somewhere lovely – in your mind. Take a few seconds to close your eyes, if safe do so. And take yourself off to the beach, a forest, a cozy fireside, a warm swimming pool, whatever scene works for you, and imagine in as much detail as you can. What can you see, hear, smell, touch, or taste in your little fantasy space?

Your brain does not differentiate between reality and this fantasy. If reality sucks in that precise moment, take a few seconds to retreat into a private, heavenly place and watch your mood improve, even if only a little.

Sniff a beautiful scent. The sense of smell is linked directly to the part of the brain that helps regulate emotions, so taking a few seconds to sniff an uplifting scent such as lemon, orange, lime, lavender, or a woody scent such as cedar, can help shift a bad mood in a better direction.

Have a chat with a friend. Share your feelings if you can. Even if you don't go into lots of detail about your feelings, you will feel better about making a connection.

Hug your husband, dog, child, best friend, or tree. Wrap your arms around yourself and hug yourself.

The above are some quick-fix solutions to help ease you out of a bad mood. None of them will give you a hangover, a DUI, or wreck a relationship, so give them a try. Practice the foundations of good health, healthy routines, and mindsets and you will be less bothered by low moods as you learn new ways to respond to them.

Before you finish the chapter today, scan back over it and chose three methods you know you can use easily next time you feel in a bad mood. You could make a short list of them and pop it onto a file on your phone or PC. The important thing is to use strategies to bust a bad mood without alcohol.

There is no reason why a bad mood should lead you back to a drink.

Summary:
- Bad moods can trigger the urge to drink, so it is important to have strategies to deal with difficult feelings when they hit.
- Aim to gently improve a mood rather than try to dramatically change it in an instant.
- Chose three strategies that you know will work for you and use one of them next time you feel in a bad mood.

Let's Celebrate!

In the last two chapters, I have talked about difficult feelings being a trigger to drink. But the opposite can also be true. Feeling happy, elated, or joyous can also nudge people towards a drink. Natalie shared her story with me which bears this out:

"I was sober about two years when my dad died unexpectedly and my marriage ended abruptly. I didn't drink and I tried hard to do all the right things to stay sober. About a year after my losses, I met a new man, got a new job, and moved abroad to a sunny location. Life was on the up. I was living the dream. During a Christmas lunch with work colleagues, I suddenly had the overpowering urge to have a glass of wine. I was happy and enjoying life more than I had done in a long time. A little voice in my head seemed to suggest that if I had a drink, it would make my happy life even happier. I was on a high and a drink seemed like a great idea at that moment."

Natalie explained how she took that drink. This led to her slipping back into her old habits of being a daily drinker. Luckily, Natalie saw all the signs of her problem drinking returning and she amended her lifestyle to become alcohol-free again. This experience has alerted Natalie. She enjoys the good times and upbeat feelings, but she is aware that feeling too 'high' can be tricky for her.

Extremes of emotion either way can upset our impulse control. When we feel calm, the logical part of the brain is working more effectively. When emotions are on an even keel, we are more likely to make decisions in line with our intentions. Our decisions are more rational. Natalie agrees that this is probably what happened to her. A heady mix of new romance, Christmas cheer, and sunshine undermined her intentions, and she drank again.

As Natalie reflected on her experience, she saw that for a couple of years before her relapse, she had been on an emotional rollercoaster. She felt she was in survival mode and was just trying to keep going. Natalie was compelled to keep moving fast and had no time for any personal reflection. She conceded that her emotions were all over the place, with no sense of emotional balance.

Keeping emotions evenly balanced is not easy. Rampaging emotions, even so-called 'good' feelings, can throw us off balance and make a drink seem like a great idea. That's why I encourage you to build in a few moments of self-reflection each day. Making this a habit is like pressing an emotional brake pedal, putting the brakes on emotions that might get the better of you.

The chapter called, *'Feeling Comfortable in Your Skin'* contains lots of ideas to help you remain more emotionally balanced. Also, in this book, I talk about the Moodometer, which is basically a mind hack. This mind hack can help keep track of emotions before they build up into an intensity that can set you off balance. So get into the habit of using the Moodometer to avoid getting overwhelmed by your emotions.

Maybe you are like Natalie and a special celebration, such as Christmas is a trigger to drink. But consider this:

Natalie was enjoying life and having a good time before she lifted a drink. You can too. Most happy occasions are happy because people are making an effort to be jolly and sociable. People have perhaps dressed specially for the occasion. There might be decorations, music, and ambient lighting. All these factors will naturally make us feel more upbeat. So focus on these rather than the drink. Alcohol might be available, but it might surprise you how many people choose to drink soft drinks.

Some years ago, I worked with a woman called Dawn, who realized that she needed to stop drinking. Her habit of drinking one or two bottles of wine every night was affecting her health, job, and relationships. Dawn was able to cut out the nightly wine but felt it would be okay to drink at Christmas. She also thought it would be okay to drink at a party or a special lunch or dinner out. Weddings, funerals, and christenings were added to the list of acceptable times to drink. Dawn had a big family and a wide circle of friends. She was active in many groups in her town. I questioned her about how often these 'special occasions' would take place. Dawn concluded that an event would happen at least once a week, possibly more. Dawn agreed that she never had just one or two drinks on her 'special' occasion. As we chatted, it became more apparent that Dawn's fantasy of a couple of drinks on the odd special occasion was just that – a fantasy. She realized that she would be back to square one, drinking every day, if she got into the habit of drinking at celebrations.

So, if you think it would work for you to save drinking for special times, take a moment, to be honest with yourself.

If you have this little loophole in your alcohol-free life, will drinking be a one-off on isolated occasions or will it creep back in and take over the show? There are no rights or wrongs here, it is about being honest with yourself and what will work for you.

Like many people, you may associate drinking with happy occasions or celebrations. The chapters in this book called *'Swapping out the Beer Goggles'* and *'From Fantasy Island to the Land of Your Dreams'* are all about challenging your thinking, beliefs, and fantasies about alcohol, so make sure you read those to help you deal with strong associations between drinking and special times. If you realize that an occasion is a big trigger for you to drink, remember to use the COPE strategy to help you deal with troubling thoughts about drinking. These thoughts might play on your mind before the event or during it. A reminder that the chapter called 'How *Are You Coping?'* is also full of strategies to use to deal with triggers to drink.

The following are some additional methods to help avoid falling into the temptation to drink during special celebrations: Always keep your 'Purpose Statement' somewhere visible to you. You will remember your Purpose Statement is your reason for wanting to be alcohol-free. Keep it as a file on your phone, a note in your diary or shorten the sentence to key letters and have them engraved on a bracelet or inked on your arm – whatever works for you. Use the statement as a reminder when your resolve is weak.

Practical approaches to help enjoy an event alcohol-free are to take a bottle of your favorite soft drink to the occasion. By doing this you have something to drink that you like. You could offer to drive, so you have a valid excuse to turn down an alcoholic drink if you feel you need an excuse. Often it helps to have a non-drinking buddy with you to support you in your efforts to avoid the booze. Lastly, always have an exit plan. This means you can go when you need to. If the temptation to drink gets overwhelming, you can leave with your sobriety intact.

To finish I will leave you with this thought: imagining that a substance that has caused you so many problems will make happy feelings *happier* or joyous occasions *more joyous* makes no sense at all. It is a fantasy.

Challenge this faulty thinking and set yourself up to enjoy celebrations you will remember with a clear conscience, a clear head, and genuine happiness.

Summary:
- So-called 'good' feelings can be triggers to drink. Intense emotion upsets our impulse control.
- Happy occasions and celebrations can also trigger drinking.
- To stay alcohol-free, it is helpful to safeguard your emotional balance and take extra care when you feel on a high.

Drawing Your Line in the Sand.

Boundaries often get a bad rap. But in this chapter, we will look at boundaries as an easy way to keep yourself safe and comfortable, which will reduce your temptation to drink. Let me explain. If we have no boundaries, or they are a bit fuzzy, life can end up being inconsistent and chaotic. We lurch from one situation to another, trying to figure things out and react as best we can, without a solid idea of what we want, what we need, or how to deal with challenges that come up.

All this stumbling about through life results in feeling anxious, uncertain, and downright stressed – classic triggers to drink alcohol. So being clear about what is right for you and moving through life with self-assurance means you show up each day with self-confidence and high self-esteem. You feel safe and comfortable because you have clarity about what you want, need, expect, and can give.

Setting boundaries means we can curate what is important to us. We are not at the mercy of other people's whims, letting others dictate what we do and how we behave. Feeling like we cannot speak up for ourselves creates resentment and passive resignation – more triggers that can lead right back to the bottle.

Many of the women I spoke to in my research for this book reported low self-confidence and self-esteem as issues that contributed to their heavy drinking. Many recognized that they were chronic people pleasers. To compound matters, many women who were practicing a program of recovery felt confused about how to balance their own needs with being of service to others. Feelings of shame, self-loathing, and hollowness persisted.

People who cannot set boundaries are often conflict-avoiders or people-pleasers, over-concerned with the feelings of others. It can be agonizingly difficult for such people to set boundaries. But if you want a healthy recovery, it needs to be done. Like most things, it gets easier with practice.

It is essential to learn how to set boundaries to get sober and stay sober. You need to be able to say 'no'. Eventually, someone will try to push a drink on you, so set boundaries now and start right away. Practice this skill so that when you find yourself in a situation where you are being urged to drink alcohol, you will be able to hold your ground.

Also, in early recovery people often feel inspired and enthused about their new lifestyle. They run around helping others, attending this or that event, and end up burnt out and resentful. This usually leads to a drink. Being clear about boundaries helps avoid this type of situation.

I saw this situation happen a lot. In an area where I used to live, there was a charitable, part government-funded program that trained people in recovery to function as peer mentors. This worked well. The peer mentors would come alongside people who were still struggling to maintain a sober life and support and counsel them. The organization, strapped for cash, was keen to harness the newly sober mentors' enthusiasm. There appeared to be no limits on how much work these mentors could put in. The big prize was to get recognition and obtain a paid job. I witnessed many of these mentors crash and burn. They were fired up with enthusiasm, burnt themselves out, and ended up drinking or using again. In their newfound zeal, they set no boundaries and they just imploded.

Don't get me wrong. I would encourage anyone to attend meetings, carry a message of recovery, and look after their health. But work out what you can realistically do and say no when you need to. This means you will have a sustainable recovery, one that will last. Put boundaries on your time and energy. In the long run, you will have more to give, not less.

A lack of boundaries among many drinkers can often be traced back to their upbringing. Frequently, their parents were too permissive or too strict. In the first situation, children learn that there are no restrictions, so they become impulsive and accustomed to instant gratification. For individuals who grow up with extremely strict parents, boundaries are experienced as rigid and tight, something to rebel against. People in this repressed situation usually can't wait to leave home and do all the stuff they were not allowed to do.

Lack of self-imposed boundaries – having whatever you want whenever you want it – leads to excess. And weak boundaries mean individuals find it difficult to accept responsibility for thoughts, attitudes, and actions

Jeanette's story illustrates how weak boundaries can hurt us and make recovery from alcohol dependence even more challenging. Jeanette had stopped drinking and started attending a woman's recovery meeting. She was a busy mother of three teenagers and worked full-time as a nurse. Her husband knew that Tuesday night was her night to attend her recovery meeting. Jeanette talked to me as she felt frustrated about her inability to get to her meeting.

As she talked it through, she realized that every Tuesday late afternoon her husband would phone or text, suggesting they go out for dinner or catch a movie or ask her to pick up one of the kids as he had to work late. Jeanette felt frustrated and perplexed by his behavior. She mused on trying to find reasons why he was doing this. After a few moments of focusing on his motivations and actions, I pointed out to her that it was her responsibility to get herself to the meeting. After a few 'buts' Jeanette agreed. She had not been clear enough about her boundaries.

That day she went home and told her family she would be out for a couple of hours every Tuesday evening and that she was unavailable. The family still tried to make suggestions for alternative activities on a Tuesday or had last-minute requests for lifts, but Jeanette stuck to her guns, and eventually, the message sank in.

Jeanette's story illustrates that boundaries are up to you. They are not about other people. It is up to you to decide what boundaries are right for you, to hold those boundaries, to communicate them to others, and to decide how you will respond if other people step over a boundary. To use Jeanette's experience as an example, it might seem that her family was trampling all over her needs and wishes. But it was up to Jeanette to reaffirm what she needed and wanted.

Initially, Jeanette blamed her family for preventing her from getting to the meeting. She was tempted to let them know how it was *their* fault she was unable to attend. But on reflection, she realized it was up to her, so she avoided blaming them.

So, boundaries are up to you. No one else will set them for you. Expect some opposition from others, especially if they have gotten used to you being overly agreeable and running around after them. When you stop, they will try to get you to go back to your old behavior because there was more in it for them. Usually, this is done unconsciously and with no malice on the part of the other person. It's just human nature. Why wouldn't they kick against not getting all that good stuff coming their way?

For many, it can be difficult to get started telling people what you want and need. Often this can be extra difficult in close relationships. You might be able to tell a waiter your meal is cold and send it back to the kitchen in a restaurant, but you just can't find the words to tell your mother you can't take all her calls while you are working.

If you are fearful of conflict in a relationship, is it due to fear that the relationship can't handle it, and you don't feel secure enough? This is an example of black-and-white thinking – if we argue we will break up. A respectful exchange of views, even a heated debate, is healthy, so don't twist yourself out of shape to avoid any conflict.

Expressing an opinion that differs from someone else does not equal a bust-up.

Boundaries can fall into two types: Firstly, those that you set for yourself. For example, "I will stop drinking." Secondly, the boundaries you set with others. For example, "I am not available for calls when I am working."

In setting a boundary on your behavior, the limits you set for yourself will guide your actions. Only you can decide what you want and what is right for you. If you cross a line you have drawn for yourself, you can review your behavior and either re-set the boundary or adjust it if you need to. For some people, setting a rule of complete abstinence is their self-imposed boundary. For others, it might be a glass of wine on a Friday night.

The boundaries you set will be based on your values and beliefs. If you are struggling to set or maintain a boundary, your boundary is at odds with a belief, and you need to reconsider or change that belief. For example, you say ''No'' to your teenage son who wants to borrow your car when you need it to get to a meeting. But then you find yourself weakening and saying ''Yes''. You then feel resentful because you missed your meeting. You might even have a drink and blame him because he took the car. You examine your beliefs and see that you hold firm to the idea that you are a selfless mother. This has gotten in the way of caring for your needs. Examine and redefine that belief. See boundary setting as part of your self-care, keeping you comfortable and safe.

If you find that others' behavior is disrespectful to your well-being, you can challenge it and respectfully re-assert your needs. When speaking with the other person, keep the focus on what you need or want. Don't blame the other person, or tell them what to do. For example, if you work at home and a friend keeps phoning you, expecting you to take all her calls, tell her you are unavailable for calls between certain hours and can't respond if she phones during this time. You are not telling her what to do. There are no recriminations or complaints. You are setting a boundary.

When dealing with others, be assertive, not aggressive. You don't need to be on the attack, just speak your truth as calmly and reasonably as you can. Don't overcomplicate or apologize. To go back to the example from earlier involving the son borrowing his mother's car when she needs it, all she needs to say is: "I need the car tonight. You can have it Thursday and Saturday nights if you want." If other people ignore what you say or keep asking for the same thing when you have said no, use the broken record technique: explain once and then repeat your phrase 'I can't ...' without any more explanation or apologies. They will eventually get the message.

Before I finish this chapter, I want to talk about a concept that happens to women a lot. It happens to men too, but in my research and experience, it is a common experience amongst women: *objectification*. Most people would understand this to mean being treated as an object – often how a woman looks. But it goes beyond this and covers situations in which you feel used or ignored.

Objects are used as tools. Maybe you have this sort of role in the family. People are used to using you as a cook, driver, host, cleaner, gardener, events manager, or dog's body. This type of situation usually isn't thought out, and it isn't necessarily devious or cruel. It's just the routine life has settled into. Being treated as an object – as a useful entity for getting things done – breeds resentment, anger, and exhaustion. A toxic mix that alcohol seems to fix – until it doesn't.

To avoid this, set some boundaries on how you are treated, whether this is at work or home. Talk to the others involved, express how you feel, list the jobs that need to be done, and divide them up with others. Sounds simple, doesn't it? It is. It is our self-doubt, self-limiting beliefs, and fear that hold us back. Many of the ideas presented in this book will help you find the self-belief and courage in yourself to establish the boundaries you need, to get well, and stay well. Boundaries are not harsh, uncaring, or divisive. They help keep you safe, cared for, and comfortable.

You might feel your only value is in how you look, and what you can do for other people, or you might have gotten used to feeling you have nothing of value to say because your contributions are overlooked or ignored. Maybe you have had an experience like this: You share an idea in a meeting at work or at home. The idea is met by silence. The idea is not even acknowledged. You cringe inwardly, thinking it must have been a rubbish idea. You learn not to speak up. Being treated this way is not acceptable. Repeat your idea at least until it is acknowledged. Again, this is a boundary that you can establish by your behavior and response to how you are treated.

A woman I know, Claudia, who comes across as confident in daily life but has struggled most of her life with issues around drinking, shared this experience with me:

''In my twenties, I started dating a man quite a bit older than me. He was very complimentary, and I thought he treated me with respect. One Saturday afternoon, we went out for a shopping trip. I needed a new outfit for a wedding we had been invited to. His brother was getting married, and he wanted to impress his brother by turning up with me, his 'stunning new girlfriend'. As usual, he took charge of the itinerary and we visited various shops in the mall. He picked out outfits and urged me to try them on. I was popping out of the changing rooms to get his opinion, which he was keen to give. I must have tried on twenty outfits that day. I went home empty-handed and feeling all wound up and angry. At the time, I wasn't exactly sure why I felt so angry. He had been so kind and said such nice things. I remember I drank about two bottles of wine that night and rang him up. I can't remember what I said, but I had a terse voicemail from him early the next day and I never saw him again.''

Looking back on that experience with more maturity and insight, Claudia realizes that he was treating her like an object. It was all wrapped up in compliments and smiles, but being objectified negates who we are on the inside, and it feels icky. No wonder she felt angry and upset. These vague, uncomfortable feelings that can be difficult to verbalize or find a reason for can lead straight to a drink.

Objectification of women happens all the time. Set boundaries to make sure it doesn't happen to you. The feelings that this type of treatment brings up could lead back to a drink. If you are ignored, repeat yourself until you are heard. If your opinion is overlooked, re-state it assertively. Look people in the eye and wait for an answer. Don't cringe and slope off, feeling bad about yourself. You don't need to feel bad, you just need to draw your line in the sand.

Don't weaken, keep going and stay well. Prioritizing your inner peace and health and saying no is not being selfish.

Summary:
- Boundaries help give us safe and comfortable. They can be flexible and adaptive.
- We can set boundaries with *ourselves*, what we will do or not do, and we can set boundaries with *other people* by being clear about what we will accept and what we will not tolerate.
- Boundaries are all about *us* as individuals. *We* set the boundary, *we* speak up as needed, and *we* establish what we want. We cannot expect other people to guess what we want or need.

Finding the Sweet Spot.

Beth and Anne agreed to meet me for a celebratory coffee and cake to mark Beth's milestone of one year sober. Both women were eager to share how sobriety had been for them so far.

"Over the past year, the trickiest aspect of sobriety has been ditching my habit of going to extremes with everything." Beth expressed this with a rueful smile, shaking her head as if perplexed.

I knew Beth when she was hitting the booze hard, and I could certainly agree that she did alcohol to the extreme. She continued:

"The people at my recovery group told me that I should eat candy to help beat cravings for drink. Maybe that is a ploy to keep me going back to their meeting. Telling me to eat sweets was music to my ears! Unfortunately, I put on about ten pounds in the first month or two, so then I got into exercise. I was running, swimming, and rollerblading every day. After a fall on the rollerblades and an injured knee from running. I had to stop that for a while and rest up. So, while I was at home, healing from a sprained wrist and a dodgy knee, I realized I was watching about 12 hours of Netflix a day. I seem to find it hard to do anything moderately, but I am slowly learning!"

"Why do you think you keep going to extremes with everything," I asked.

Beth took a few seconds to answer and sighed, "I guess I'm constantly looking for a high, I suppose."

I listened as Beth went on to explain that she was aware of her need to seek thrills and heightened feelings. It was as if enough was never enough for her.

"The sugar, alcohol, and exercise all give me a rush that I get hooked on. I genuinely thought I was doing good with all the exercise and considered the endorphins to be healthy and made me feel good." Beth shrugged her shoulders and laughed.

"So, what was Netflix doing for you?" I was keen to find out her take on this.

"I was watching back-to-back thrillers and horrors. I think I got hooked on the adrenalin"

I was aware Beth had a difficult childhood. She grew up in a tough neighborhood, with violent alcoholic parents who regularly fought and smashed the house up. As a child, Beth was on high alert, twenty-four-seven, and this state of anxiety and fear meant she was inclined to seek thrills to maintain this heightened state. Beth had grown up accustomed to chaos, drama, and heightened stimulation, and she continued to seek out substances and behaviors to take to the extreme. For Beth, doing anything moderately felt boring and flat. She had to learn to adapt to a calm life without so many highs and lows.

Beth looked at me earnestly and said: "I have learned my lesson, you know. It frightened me. When I was at home recuperating from my injuries, I started thinking about how good it would be to have a drink to cope with being on my own at home and take the edge of the pain. That was a wake-up call for me."

During the exchange, Anne was nodding her head, with an animated smile.

"Yes, with me it was work." She exclaimed.

Anne proceeded to share how she had a new job as a teacher three months into her newfound sobriety. Anne was spending every evening and all her weekends marking students' work and preparing meticulously for lessons. She stopped attending the sobriety meetings that she had initially found so helpful. Anne was neglecting to eat properly or get out for some fresh air and exercise. She struggled to sleep and began drinking again in a futile effort to switch off her busy brain at night. Anne feels she has learned a valuable lesson from this experience.

"I just wasn't looking after myself. I was taking work to extremes and got quite ill." After a pause, Anne continued: "I had to have an honest heart-to-heart with my Headteacher who was understanding. I have a job share now and decided my sobriety was worth some financial sacrifices."

I asked Anne and Beth what had helped them find some balance in their lives. Both agreed that making self-care a priority in their lives was necessary. Beth commented that she realized she only has a certain amount of energy and time in a day, and she has to decide how to use it wisely. She went on to say:

"For me, it is about deciding what is most important to me and focusing on doing a few things well and in moderation. If I get tired or start to feel overwhelmed, I pull back on my commitments and rest. It has been trial and error, but I am getting better at it."

Anne shared that she found the acronym H.A.L.T to be helpful. (Hungry, Angry, Lonely, Tired.) She avoided letting herself get too hungry, angry, lonely, or tired. She would eat, talk to someone, or rest if she started to feel uncomfortable. With a laugh, Anne commented: "It is not rocket science. But I can make life very complicated for myself!"

Both Anne's and Beth's stories illustrate that even when the drink is put down, the behavior of taking things to extremes can continue. Working hard or exercising might seem like worthwhile activities, but if they are pursued beyond endurance, they become problematic. The propensity to behave in this obsessive way shows more work is needed in recovery. In addition, the consequent stress or pain that such behavior creates could make alcohol seem attractive and so undermine physical sobriety.

What is the answer? For me, it is helpful to visualize all the areas in my life as buckets with labels for each aspect of my current existence. I have buckets each labeled with the following:

- Health
- Marriage and family
- Friends
- Community
- Work
- Hobbies/Fun stuff

Pretty self-explanatory – but the problem with my buckets is that they have holes in them. I aim to ensure the buckets are all getting nicely topped up, avoiding any one of them from running dry. I fill up the buckets with my energy, effort, and attention. Each bucket needs attention. Sometimes one might need more than another, depending on what is going on in my life. For example, a little while ago I had multiple family bereavements within a year. The rapid succession of losses hit me hard. During this time, I paid particular attention to my health, community, friends, hobbies, and family. I eased up on pouring lots of attention and energy into the working bucket and just did what I had to keep things ticking over. At other times in life, such as when I was studying for a professional qualification, I needed to put lots of time, energy, and attention into the working bucket – but I kept an eye on the others to make sure they were all kept topped up.

This analogy of the buckets works for me. For other people, thinking of each area in life as a section in a pie, a spoke in a wheel, or part of a plate can help. The point is to ensure that no area is neglected and there is a sense of all areas of life jogging along happily in equal measure.

A visual analogy like the ones above might work for you. Some other people prefer a grid system. You can draw up boxes on a sheet of paper and label each one with headings like my bucket labels. You then could put in a score out of ten in each box – ten being very satisfied and zero being extremely unsatisfied. Then, based on your scores, evaluate which sections of life need your attention to achieve balance. If a section has a low score that means I am feeling out of whack with that aspect of my life and

I need to put some effort into improving the situation. For example, if I gave my 'Marriage and family Life' a low score, I would make sure I planned some enjoyable things to do with my family in the next week or so.

Choose a visual or recorded method that works for you. I call this my *Balance Sheet.*

You might wonder whether it's worth the bother. Well, if life gets all out of whack, it can get uncomfortable and painful. For most of us, pain and discomfort are triggers to drink and are not worth the risk.

You might ask, "Okay, I need to work on balance in my life. How do I know when I need to adjust before it gets too late?"

This is a great question. The answer is *paying attention.* In practical terms, this means having a system of reviewing your life balance. You could use the following: The first step is to make a list of the areas in your life, such as work, family, social life, and so on. Your list will be individual to you. Write a list on paper or type it into a note on your phone. The next step is to look at the list and use the visuals or the grid system to quantify each area. For example, I do this every Sunday evening when I am planning for the week ahead. I look at my list of headings for each area and reflect on the previous week by asking myself a few questions. I don't necessarily write everything down but will make a few notes on what I need to do in the week ahead. It might look like this:

Health – How have my energy levels been? Have I managed to engage in some movement each day, without overdoing it? Have I eaten healthily and in moderation?

Have I rehydrated regularly? Do I have any health checks that need to be booked? Am I feeling optimistic and enjoying my days?

Marriage and family – Have I had time with my husband just to enjoy each other's company? Are there any family issues that need to be addressed? Have I communicated with all my close family this week, how has that been? Are there any special anniversaries, celebrations, or birthdays coming up this week?

Friends – Have I spent time with friends this week? Are any special dates coming up? Am I neglecting any friends or giving too much to others? Have I got a balance between social time with others and alone time?

Community – Have I engaged with my local community this week? Do I have online communities to tap into, and have I interacted with them?

Work – How many hours have I worked this week? Am I enjoying work? (See below for more about this. Work is an area which can become very unbalanced in many people's lives)

Hobbies/Fun stuff – Do I have a range of interests that get me out and away from a screen? Do I have a balance of chill-out activities, such as TV or light reading, and more active pursuits that require a bit of mental or physical effort? Am I trying new activities? What can I plan to have something to look forward to? Am I enjoying all my activities and if not, what can I do about that?

Your labels might be different. You might have children, education, finances, life planning, personal development, and spirituality. It all depends on your priorities and your stage in life. So don't feel confined to the labels I have used or suggested.

Over the years I have used journals, calendars, and notebooks to record my reflections and plans. I have also used notes in a file on my PC or phone. You could start in whatever way is easiest for you, today. Open a file on your computer or phone and jot down a few notes. Nothing fancy. The important thing here is to do it.

This weekly review and planning take just a few minutes and is a revealing activity. I enjoy doing it. I don't like to drift through life, and this sort of exercise helps me feel more on top of things. I worry less and don't get anxious about things I might have forgotten. It helps to overcome that feeling of being overwhelmed with lots of little, niggly details floating around in my mind.

It helps to ensure I am keeping track and adjusting as needed. This means annoying situations – such as developing a health condition due to neglecting diet or exercise (or just feeling rotten) or suddenly feeling emotionally spent – are less likely to creep up unexpectedly.

I find that I need to manage my energy levels carefully. This is part of self-care. I think of energy as being like a piece of elastic. I can stretch my energy and make it go a bit further by doing activities that help build up a feeling of vitality. I minimize demands that make me feel tired. For example, after a gentle walk or ten minutes of stretching, I feel revived. So, I include plenty of walks and stretching in my day-to-day routine. Other activities, such as shopping in a large mall, I find tiring, so I minimize these.

The time of day, time of the month for women who menstruate, and the seasons in the year have an impact on energy levels. I know I am a morning person, so I do jobs that require high energy or lots of concentration early in the day. I also plan important tasks then, to make sure they get done. I have an artist friend who does her best work between 9 pm and 2 am, so she works then and sleeps later in the morning. We all have different rhythms, so pay attention to your energy levels and plan your day around them as best you can. I once had a job that involved evening and night shifts. This did not work for me, and I constantly felt like I had jet lag. I made it a priority to change jobs as it was affecting me so dramatically. Fatigue can be a big trigger to drink, so take it seriously and guard your energy as a precious resource.

Are you an introvert, extrovert, or ambivert? Introverts typically enjoy time alone and feel better after some alone time. They get tired of being with people too much. So, introverts need time alone to make sure they have as much energy as possible. The opposite is true for extroverts – they thrive on company and for them, being solitary burns up their energy. Ambiverts are somewhere in the middle. Most people are ambiverts, so the takeaway here is to (hey you are there ahead of me?) find a balance.

The last suggestion I have for maximizing your energy is this: *focus on the slow burn rather than the heavy lifting*. For example, lifting the grocery shopping out of the car. I used to go for it and pick up as many bags in one go as I could manage. I would run along into the house, straining to carry the weight and dump it all down breathlessly onto the counter. I learned that lifting a few bags out at a time worked better. No pulled muscles or sudden dips in energy. Another example is meeting deadlines. Avoid the fire-up-your-backside scenario. Some people claim they do their best work under pressure. Maybe. But for someone who wants to avoid relapsing, it is a gamble. The stress of a deadline could push you towards a drink. So, plan as much as you can to meet deadlines calmly.

At the beginning of the book, I talked about sobriety being a bit like a minefield. The mines are the triggers that could set you off on a drinking spree. You need to be able to navigate through the minefield to avoid a mine blowing up in your face. Having balance in life is a way to avoid stepping on one of these mines. Paying attention to energy levels and triggers is a way of flagging up the mines that could destroy your sobriety.

So, find the sweet spot for each area in your life and make sobriety easy and stress-free.

Summary:
- Many people who have issues with overdoing the booze, seem to overdo many other things too. Moderation and balance don't come naturally to them.
- You have finite amounts of energy. You can plan how to approach all the demands in your life and maintain energy levels. This will avoid the exhaustion and overwhelm that can lead to a drink.

- Be aware of your traits that lead to exhaustion and overwhelm such as being constantly busy, taking on too much, being a people pleaser, or leaving tasks to the last minute. Be mindful of the activities that sap your energy and those that revitalize you. Try to minimize the energy-zappers and include the energy-givers.

How Not to Relapse.

Most of us live in a culture in which alcohol is in most places and situations: cafes, bars, restaurants, on TV, on advertising billboards, and in supermarkets and food stores. It is part of most celebrations and social occasions. So having a passing thought about having a drink is just that – a passing thought – so don't get wound up about it but be vigilant. Use 'COPE' to help you deal with craving thoughts. You will find details of the COPE strategy in Part I of this book. It is covered in the chapter *The Most Important Distance You will Ever Travel.* Also, the first chapter of this part of the book, called *How Are You Coping?* gives lots of practical ideas on dealing with cravings. So if triggers or cravings for alcohol are bothering you (which they will from time to time) re-read those chapters.

Sometimes, so-called drinking dreams bother people. They don't want to drink but have a dream in which they are drinking. Again, this is normal. If you drank for years, these memories will be in your subconscious and might fuel the odd dream here and there. Having passing thoughts or dreams you can't control is quite different from fixating on the idea that you want to drink. So let the passing thoughts inspire you to do something to further solidify your recovery, such as read some literature that you use to help stay sober, go to a meeting, or talk to a sober friend.

Why do relapses occur?

Relapses can occur for all sorts of reasons including disappointments, upset, feeling like you are 'cured' of any drinking problem you might have had, or thinking negatively about yourself. Alternatively, you might feel tempted to drink when you feel on a high. There might be triggers such as certain people, places, events, or occasions that you know will be tricky for you, so it's worth working out what these are for you and being prepared.

One of the biggest underlying causes of relapse is just *feeling deprived* of a drink, feeling like you are missing out. Sometimes people might blame an upsetting event or loss as the cause of their relapse. But, deep down, a desire to drink is there already because they see alcohol as a treat they have given up. A way to avoid this pitfall is to remind yourself regularly that you have not *given up* alcohol you are *free* of alcohol. You are free of hangovers, alcohol-related health problems, unmanageable finances, rocky relationships, and the rest.

I have known people who have started drinking again, sometimes after many years, not because life was going sour but the complete opposite: life was good and they thought it was safe to drink again, bringing all the old chaos back into their lives. They drank again because, even after all that time, there was a niggling thought that somehow life would be even better with a drink. It wasn't.

What are the signs of a relapse?

The first stage of relapse is what's known as an emotional relapse. The signs that an emotional relapse might be starting is when your self-care starts to slip, and you begin neglecting the good habits that you put in place to stay away from drinking.

Another indicator is if you start feeling sorry for yourself.

And if the reason for your self-pity is simply that you're feeling sorry for yourself because you haven't had a drink, think of all the benefits that not drinking is bringing you: better physical health, better relationships, more money in your bank account, and less worry. You could make a list as soon as you have read this chapter.

The next stage is a mental relapse.

You will recognize a mental relapse when thoughts about drinking keep popping randomly into your head. Sheelagh shared the details of her mental relapse with me as follows:

"After a couple of months of not drinking, I was bothered by ideas that kept flashing across my mind. For example, I was alone in the staff kitchen at work. I spotted a bottle of wine given to the team by a customer. I suddenly thought, "I could have that. No one would miss it." Another example happened when I was in a queue at the supermarket. A special wine promotion caught my eye. "Oh, that's cheap," I thought. "I could get that." Luckily, I didn't drink the wine at work or buy the special promotion. I phoned my sponsor instead."

Sheelagh dealt with her relapse thoughts by phoning someone. This worked for her. She had the thoughts, but she didn't relapse. Talking through any thoughts you might have about drinking will work for you too. So, if you do have thoughts such as "One won't hurt" or "I deserve a drink", talk to a sober friend or mentor right away and get those thoughts out of your head. Otherwise, they could just build up into a full-blown relapse.

Another effective way of dealing with these sorts of thoughts is to question them. For instance, if you think, "I can have a drink and I'll just change to a soft drink later on", question that. Ask yourself, in your drinking past, how often did that happen? How often could you start drinking alcohol and then switch to a soda or fruit juice? If the answer is that it's never happened in the past, it's never going to happen in the future either.

If you have a thought pop into your mind that says," You can have a drink! You can stop anytime, just have one." Without shame or blame, honestly recall how alcohol affected your life. To avoid feeling deprived, you could take some time to do something nice for yourself or buy yourself a small treat with the money you have saved by not drinking. Sometimes when people do the math and work out how much they were spending on booze, it's a pleasant surprise to know that there is all this extra money available now to spend on other alcohol-free treats and activities, so make sure to do something nice for yourself.

The final stage of relapse is a physical relapse. That's when you have a drink. The longer you continue drinking, the deeper the relapse becomes and the more difficult it will be to get back. Later in this chapter, I will explain how to do a Relapse Prevention Plan. That will help you to limit any damage done and get back to a place of safe sobriety as soon as possible.

If you are reading this at a time when you have had a recent relapse – well done for getting back. Even if you are starting from day one for the tenth or one-hundredth time, stay focused on what you are doing right today and look ahead to a positive alcohol-free future. You can do this.

Your Relapse Recovery Plan

I once knew someone, who had not drunk for over a year. Due to various personal circumstances, including debt and job problems that she had told no one about, she had a relapse. This relapse involved a copious amount of alcohol, a DUI, and a failed suicide attempt, which she had no recollection of. She woke up in a police cell. This incident changed the course of her life.

There are many lessons to learn from this woman's experience and actions. If she had prepared a Relapse Recovery Plan she might have stopped at one glass, tipped the rest of the booze down the sink, and phoned a sober friend. If she had done that her life today would look quite different.

In recovery, it is helpful to let go of all-or-nothing thinking. This can apply to many areas in life, but letting go of this thinking is significant when it comes to relapse. Don't think ''Oh I've had a drink; I might as well have the bottle.'' If you do have a drink, get rid of the bottle as soon as you can, and look at your Relapse Recovery Plan.

So, what will your plan contain? Your plan will be brief but specific. If you have relapsed, you won't be in the mood to read a long rambling piece of prose. So, keep it short and to the point.

The plan will have the following headings:

1. Who will you contact within 12 hours of the relapse?
2. What will you read/listen to/engage in within the first 24 hours after the relapse?
3. What face-to-face contact or connection will you make within 48 hours?
4. What self-care will you do for yourself each day in the first week after the relapse?
5. What will you change to help avoid another relapse?

Having someone to contact within 12 hours is crucial. Phone them or see them as soon as you can. Even if you have temporarily forgotten, they will remind you why you wanted to stop drinking and of all the benefits you have had from not drinking. Sharing your thoughts with someone is key. It was your thinking that led to a drink, so you need to tap into someone else's thinking to get straight again.

Don't let shame or embarrassment hold you back. That person will be relieved you have phoned promptly. Much better to get a phone call from you after just one drink than to hear a story at a later point about your drunken accident, fight, or worse.

It might be helpful to have two or more people to contact This way you have more of a chance of catching someone. The last thing you want is an excuse to drink more because your person was unavailable. So have a few names to be sure you will have someone to talk to. Tell the person or people on your list that you would like to contact them in the event of a relapse. Explain that you are not planning a relapse but want to have an insurance plan just in case, to minimize the damage a relapse might cause.

What will you read/absorb in the first 24 hours? You might have a book or some literature that you find the motivation to get back on track. An app like Sober Grid or online inspiration will help you get back into the sober groove. Some people like Pinterest and keep a board of quotes and links to sites and literature that reminds them of how great sobriety is. Our site WinsPress.com has lots of free resources and information about books that will help you. Many people find listening to our podcasts, *The Alcohol Recovery Show*, a terrific way to keep motivated. So, list whatever you find most helpful, inspiring, and above all accessible on your plan for a relapse. Go to the material promptly and immerse yourself in it.

Online support is helpful but seeing someone or a group face to face is powerful. If you have a therapist, sponsor, sober coach, or recovery group, try to see them within 48 hours of the relapse. Be honest with them. In this way, you will get the support and guidance you need.

Each day, pay special attention to your essential self-care: decent food, adequate hydration, sleep, and movement. Write down in your plan what you will do. For example, I will get up at 7 am, I will get out for a 20-minute walk, I will eat breakfast, and I will take half an hour to relax. Write down the times that work for you. It is your plan, so write down what you know realistically will work for you.

Within that first week, with the help of the people you connect with for support, work out what happened. Were there any signs of relapse? What triggered you? What do you need to change to minimize the chances of it happening again?

Last point here before I finish. Don't let shame hold you back. Relapses happen. It is not a sign of moral failure. If you have prepared and written your plan and stopped the relapse before it turned into a major disaster, you will have shown many positive qualities, including a willingness to take responsibility, determination, and resilience. So often, I have seen how shame and embarrassment have eaten away at people and led them right back to a drink. Don't let that happen to you.

Summary:

- Relapses do happen but they are not inevitable. Make a plan so you can deal quickly with a relapse if it happens to you.
- Be aware of the signs of relapse (emotional, mental, and physical) Take pre-emptive action.
- Do not let shame hold you back from getting help if you do relapse. Look at it as a source of information and learn from the relapse.

Pulling It All Together.

A huge thank you for staying with me this far. I hope that you have been able to put some of the strategies I suggest into place in your life. This last chapter in this part of the book is a quick summary of what I have covered in Part One and Part Two of the book. Use this summary as an aide memoir.

In this chapter, I include a brief revision of each point of the plan and also some prompts you may wish to use for your self-reflection time that I encourage you to have each day. The questions are there as an aid, not a demand, so use them as you wish. Lastly in this chapter, I remind you of the action points that I have suggested you do. This is to help make it easier to ensure all the actions are carried out. This will maximize the effectiveness of the plan.

Coming up first is a quick walk-through of the plan. At each point of the plan, I have included where to find the content relating to it. Reference to each of the relevant chapters is in the brackets. Therefore, you refresh your memory if needed by re-reading those sections.

The Plan:
1. Have a plan. The chances of relapsing are high without a plan. (*Part One: Find Your Why?*)
   - Be clear about your 'why' – Complete your 'Purpose Statement' and keep it handy.
   - The basics of the plan are:

TREAT (What To Do)

Treat your body well

Reflect on your actions

Enjoy an activity

Absorb uplifting content

Talk to a trusted friend

2. Follow the plan every day, especially when you don't feel like it. That's when you need it most.

    •   Carry out the TREAT actions every day. Create a schedule to make sure you build in time to: Treat your body well. Reflect, Enjoy a rewarding activity, Absorb uplifting or inspiring content, and Talk to a trusted friend – *every* day. *(Part One: When To Do It)*

3. Treat yourself well. Be kind to your body and mind. *(Part One: Stop Beating Yourself Up.)*

    •   Include activities in your daily routine that you find soothing and relaxing

    •   Remember you are getting sober to enjoy life not to endure it.

    •   Set healthy boundaries for yourself and others. *(Part Two: Drawing Your Line in the Sand)*

    •   Aim for balance across the different areas of your life *(Part Two: Finding the Sweet Spot)*

4. Absorb uplifting books or audio content to keep you motivated. Read, listen, or watch every day.

    •   Be selective about what you watch, read, look at and listen to. Guard your mind. *(Re-read any chapter in this book.)*

- Focus on content that supports your efforts to be alcohol-free and makes you feel good. (At the WinsPress.com website you can find out about other books to help you stay alcohol-free and deal with anxiety, stress, or troubling emotions. The podcast **The Alcohol Recovery Show,** which I co-host with Lewis David, has helped thousands of people to get and stay motivated on their sober journey. You can find the podcast at WinsPress.com/podcast.)

5. Self-reflect and grow. Learn new skills and develop new attitudes. Be open to change.

- Learn skills to deal with triggers to drink. Use the COPE strategy to challenge craving thoughts. *(Part One: The Most Important Distance You Will Ever Travel)*

- Build a daily habit of self-reflection. (Part Two: Feeling Comfortable in Your Skin. In addition, there are questions for reflection in the next chapter.)

- Be aware of fantasy thinking. Use your imagination to visualize a sober and happy you. (*From Fantasy Island to The Land of Your Dreams)*

- Work on changing beliefs that are holding you back from being alcohol-free. (*Swapping Out the Beer Goggles*)

- Build resilience to cope with life *(Part Two: Bouncing Back)*

6. Enjoy an activity you like as a reward every day. Play and take pleasure in life. *(Part Two: Playing the Game)*

   - People who build in regular rewards and small treats are more motivated to get sober and stay that way.
   - Build in time to play and enjoy life

7. Talk to a trusted friend or friends.

   - Have a phone call or meet up with at least one trusted friend every day. Make efforts to create and maintain strong bonds with loved ones, friends, and the community. *(Part One: Peeps, Pals, and Playmates)*

8. Be aware of your thinking around triggers to drink and learn strategies to deal with them.

   - Use COPE to deal with craving thoughts (Part One: The Most Important Distance You Will Ever Travel; Par Two: How Are You Coping?)

9. Deal with disturbing emotions, whether these are from your past, present, or worries about the future. *(Part Two: Grab a Flashlight* and *Feeling Comfortable in Your Skin)*

   - Treat yourself with compassion (*Part One: Stop Beating Yourself Up*)
   - Make sure you are attending to your physical well-being – eating, moving, sleeping, hydrating, and relaxing. If you have slipped into poor habits get back to basics with 'Feel Great in 8': 8 hours of sleep, 8 portions of fruit/vegetables, 8 glasses of water, walk 8,000 steps, and for at least 8 minutes

sit and do absolutely nothing. Do this every day for 8 days and see if your moods improve.

- Keep track of your moods. Aim to gently improve a mood rather than have dramatic changes in how you feel. *(Part two: The Moodometer)*
- Learn to experience emotions, let them run their course, and know they will pass, no matter how intense. *(Part One: Getting Your Feelings Back)*
- In the early days, plan carefully for celebrations and be aware that feeling intensely happy can be a trigger to drink for many people. *(Part Two: Let's Celebrate)*

Questions to consider during your reflection time:

Some people are naturally thoughtful and reflective. They like to read, ponder, and meditate on aspects of their life. If you have a spiritual practice or tradition that requires personal reflection, I wholeheartedly urge you to keep that up.

But for some other folks, personal reflection does not come easily. It is a skill that can be learned. It doesn't need to be complicated or esoteric. It can be practical. The following are a few prompts and questions to use during your reflection time if needed.

- Reflect on how you are applying TREAT (**Treat** your body well. **Reflect** on your actions, **Enjoy** and activity. **Absorb** uplifting content, and **Talk** to a friend)
- Have you spotted yourself over-reacting or taking things personally? What can you learn from these

situations? *(Part 2: Feeling Comfortable in Your Skin)*

- How are you coping with bad moods or difficult emotions? Are you using the Moodometer and a range of strategies to deal with a bad mood? *(Part 2: The Moodometer and Busting a Bad Mood)*
- Are resentments or anger about the past troubling you? *(Part 2: Grab a Flashlight)*
- Are you clear about what is of value to you in your life? Do your actions line up with upholding these values? *(Part 2: Grab a Flashlight)*
- Are you setting boundaries for yourself and others? Are you sticking to them? Which ones are difficult for you to keep? *(Part 2: Drawing Your Line in the Sand)*
- Are you finding time to enjoy yourself each day and play? *(Part 2: Playing the Game)*
- Do you feel the different areas of your life are balanced? *(Part 2: Finding the Sweet Spot)*

I include these prompts for self-reflection, not as added pressure. Use what appeals to you and what you find useful.

The next section coming up is another gathering up of all the small exercises I have suggested throughout the book. Again, please don't feel pressurized. Do what you can.

Do bear in mind, though, that you will have more chance of remaining alcohol-free if you do the actions rather than just read about them.

The 9 Action Points

The following is a summary of the nine practical exercises I have explained in Part One and Part Two of this book. You may already have completed some or all of them. This is a checklist to ensure you don't miss any out. Ideally, you will write them down. By completing these exercises and recording them, you can refer back to them and chart your progress. Just reading and thinking about them makes much less impact. So, if you haven't done any of the exercises, make a start today and complete one or two each day over the next week or so.

1. Write your **'Purpose Statement'** (notes on how to do this are in Part 1: Find Your Why.)
2. Complete the **Changing Beliefs** exercise (explained in Part One: Swapping Out the Beer Goggles.)
3. Make up your **TREAT Schedule**. (Instructions on doing this are in Part One: When to Do IT.)
4. Write down your **list of strategies to deal with stress and triggers.** (There are lots of suggested strategies in the chapters How Are You Coping? Grab a Flashlight and Bouncing Back.)
5. Complete the **Resilience Tracker**: Re-do this at intervals to chart your progress and see where you can improve. *(You can remind yourself how to do this in Part 2: Bouncing Back.)*
6. Put together a **list of activities you can turn to when tempted to drink**. Better still, prepare a box of goodies to enjoy when you are assailed by temptation. *(I suggest some ideas in Part Two, How Are You Coping.)*

7. To help shift a bad mood choose three activities that work for you and make a list to turn to when you need it. *(I suggest some ideas in Part 2: Busting a Bad Mood)*

8. Regularly complete a Balance Sheet to review how you are balancing your efforts across the different parts of your life. *(I explain how to do a 'Balance Sheet in Part 2: Finding the Sweet Spot)*

9. Write your **Relapse Prevention Plan** *(Part 2: How Not to Relapse)*

In the last section of the book coming up next, I cover some common questions people have about stopping drinking. So, if any questions have popped into your mind as you have been reading, hopefully, they will be addressed there. If not, please feel free to contact me at the WinsPress site via the contact page. I would love to hear from you.

Also, in the final part of the book, I talk about some of the social issues that women face and how these impact our relationship with alcohol. Knowing a little about this social context might help to keep you motivated, so do read on.

PART
THREE.

Freedom?

I was recently on holiday, visiting family and friends in my hometown. I spent a warm, sunny September morning walking around the harbor area of the town with my brother. In common with many harbor towns, there is no shortage of bars. As we passed a historical building with a lively crowd sitting outside enjoying the sunshine, my brother recounted a story about a female friend who had trouble buying an alcoholic drink in this bar simply because she was alone. Our feminist feathers were ruffled. I tutted and shook my head. What an outrage. In this day and age, such blatant discrimination is unacceptable.

It got me thinking.

Not so long ago in Britain, it was illegal to serve a woman on her own an alcoholic drink. This law only changed in 1982. I can *remember* 1982. I was shocked at only how recently the law had changed.

I was a teenager in the 1980s. I wasn't aware of this recent change to legislation at the time, but I *was* conscious of the freedom I felt I had at the time. I remember my attitude seemed to shock my mother. She was pretty much tee-total – literally, she drank gallons of tea. I remember she explained her distaste for alcohol by recounting a story of mild inebriation and consequent nausea as a result of drinking too many cherry liquors. 'Lightweight' I thought disparagingly, with all my teenage wisdom.

Her lack of experience with drinking contrasted with the drinking culture I was quickly immersed in as I entered young adulthood. Not only was I grown-up, but I was also a grown-up woman – who could drink. The female generation that preceded mine seemed tame, downtrodden, domesticated, and *sober*. We were wild, free, living life to the full.

Going to bars, clubs, and pubs felt like progress, freedom, equality, and rebellion. I felt like I was sticking up two fingers to the patriarchy. The old fogeys weren't going to hold us girls back. We would be there with the lads, pints in hand, matching them drink for drink. We scoffed at the drinks our mothers favored, such as sherry or sweet liquors, sticking to pints of beer, cider, or spirits such as vodka and whiskey. Drinking was an expression of independence and self-determination.

In my family, I was the first woman to get a university degree and I was probably the first woman in my family to drink a pint of beer or go into a pub alone. Having the 'right' to drink as men felt like an exercise in liberty. Flexing a bicep to lift a pint was liberating, fun, and a symbol of 'girl-power'.

My experience has been echoed in the responses I have had from numerous women during my interviews with podcast listeners and readers. A woman, Lyn, summed up her recollections in an email to me:

''I rebelled when I became a teenager and the messages in the 90s were all about ladette culture, secret drinks with friends to be cool and fit in with an in-crowd became the norm. When I entered relationships, it became about going out, and the clubs we frequented were either discounted drinks at members' clubs or 'pound-a-pint night'. I had a 'let's try to get my money's worth attitude'. Later on, drinking with a partner over meals increased. We went to France, where wine was cheaper than water, and we always brought carloads back with us, which made it even more tempting to drink.''

Fast forward to the 2020s and female-themed alcohol memes, greeting cards, slogans, pink drinks, mugs, and references to 'mummy-juice'. Saturday brunches advertised with bottomless bubbly are popular in the city close to me, and spa treats with 'bubbles' are commonplace. My goth-inclined teenage self would be horrified at the sparkling, pastel-colored alcoholic beverages pushed our way. But one thing is clear: the advertisers for the drinks industry have tapped into the female enthusiasm for booze. Nowadays, it seems like the market is saturated with pink fizz. We girls are encouraged to gulp, giggle, and enjoy – what's the harm?

This freedom to drink with the boys, exercised by my generation and all those girls and women after me with such gusto, has a price tag. There are many price tags, including health, self-esteem, relationships, and more.

The alcohol industry advertisers have latched on to our taste for freedom in a bottle and capitalized on our thirst for equality. You might think you are not influenced by advertising, but let's pause for a few moments to consider the power these images, jingles, concepts, and fantasies have over us.

The most effective advertising strategies are those that work the most subtly. Have you ever found yourself humming a catchy little tune after hearing a jingle? It has wormed its way into your consciousness without you even realizing it. Psychologists have run experiments to show that the more we are exposed to an image, a person, a tune, or a product, and the more familiar it becomes to us, the more likely we will be to bring it into our lives. About alcohol, you may have had the thought of a particular drink flash into your mind and wonder, 'Where did that come from?' only to realize at a later point you had driven past a billboard with an ad for that drink, earlier in the day. These images can just be on the edge of our consciousness, but they can affect our thinking powerfully, especially when we are busy and preoccupied with other more pressing matters.

In past decades, alcohol advertisements were aimed at men, often using women as objects to make alcohol appear glamorous and appealing to men. As alcohol sales to men have gone down, the ad people turned their attention to a group of people who now had more education, better jobs, and equal pay and were ready to get out there and whoop it up with the boys. The liberated working woman needed to uncork a bottle of the red stuff to relax after a hectic day running after the kids or running a corporation.

If you have not noticed alcohol-related ads directed at women, the following is a quick overview of some of the more odious adverts for items I've come across: Ads for jewelry that conceals a mini flask to stash booze. Beer with a pink label with a little black dress on it (the obsession with pink is nauseating!) An in-shower wineglass holder. (It is impossible to enjoy a bath or shower without alcohol.) Self-care and relaxation have become inextricably entwined with booze. There's skinny vodka because we women all want to be skinny and drink like the lads. And in 2018, the drinks company that sells the famous *Johnnie Walker* brand of whiskey launched its 'feminist' label: *Jane Walker*.

And it's not just advertising. Television has a big role to play too. TV programs have also reflected and intensified these social trends. In many TV programs, women who are presented as successful, glamorous, and empowered are pictured with a glass of alcohol in their hands at regular intervals. Think about *The Good Wife*, *Suits*, and *Grey's Anatomy*. The linkage is clear.

Like all advertising, these images, gimmicks, and products are selling a fantasy. The fantasies include the empowered young woman, working and playing hard, and relaxing with brightly colored cocktails in glamorous bars with fashionable friends. Another delusion presented to us is the array of wines, artisan gins, and beers that prove we have cultured tastes and a sophisticated lifestyle. Of course, there is the ubiquitous 'mummy juice' or 'mummy's little helper' – alcohol to shore up the flagging energies of the harassed mother.

This trend follows the same pattern as another substance: tobacco. I will refer to this briefly, as there are interesting parallels with alcohol. In the early days advertising tobacco was aimed very much at men. Then some bright spark in the advertising industry realized they were missing out on at least half of the population. Cigarette advertising then became focused on women – bring on the *Virginia Slims*, a female-orientated fashion brand aimed at 18- to 35-year-olds. The themes of the advertising campaign were, independence, liberation, slimness, glamour, style, and taste. Sound familiar?

The advertisers want us to think we are in control, that we are making the decisions. We might decide to have red or white wine, or after some thought go for the prosecco and not the rose. But are we in control when we pour the fourth drink or open that second or third bottle of wine? At the end of a night's drinking, are we really 'deciding' to ring our ex-husband to tell him what we think of him? Who is in control when we stagger home alone, late on a Saturday night?

Can you think of any other situation in which you would agree to lose the power of clear thinking, coherent speech, and rational decisions and risk injury or attack? Oh, and in addition, hand over your hard-earned cash for the privilege of embarrassing or hurting yourself. No, me neither. But, when you think about it in these terms, that is what we are doing when we acquiesce to the ad people: we abandon our autonomy and endanger our health.

In my experience of talking with women who have decided to stop drinking, many of them have dark, lurid tales of situations that were dangerous, degrading, or repulsive to them. Women who look conspicuously drunk are targets for predatory men. The whole issue of predatory men is a systemic, societal problem that should be dealt with in its own right. The woman is not to blame.

Sadly, that's the society we live in. We need to keep ourselves safe. Is it safe to get into a taxi with an unknown man to go to his flat? Would you let a strange male get intimate with you in a public space if you had just had tea that evening? Who is in control of these situations? Who is making the decisions? It isn't the woman who has just down the tenth Jane Walker or imbibed six bottles of beer featuring the pink label and little black dress.

The illusion of control, fun, glamour, glitz, or relaxation is just that, an illusion. The reality can be stark, depressing, dangerous, and degrading. Let's see past the hype and look at the unglamorous and ugly truth.

The statistics would indicate that more and more women are drinking in a way that is hurting them – physically, emotionally, and psychologically. (https://www.cdc.gov/alcohol/fact-sheets/womens-health.htm) Nearly half of adult women reported drinking in the past 30 days. 13% of women report binge drinking 4 times a month. In 2019 32% of female high school, students consumed alcohol compared to 26% of male high school students. In 2019 8% of women aged 18 to 25 years had an alcohol use disorder. Advertising must have a massive role to play in these statistics.

In recent years there has been a powerful shift. Increasing numbers of women are wondering if alcohol has not liberated them but shackled them. In 2016 Kirsti Coulter posted an essay on how big tech was pressuring women employees to drink. The #MeToo movement has also been a significant influence, as it has highlighted sexual harassment and assault with alcohol very much center stage. Increasing numbers of influencers, celebrities, and women in the public eye are canceling alcohol and announcing their intention to stop drinking.

The recent movie *Promising Young Woman* reflects this massive social shift. The main character, a young woman called Cassie, sets out to get revenge on predatory men who violate women who have been served too much alcohol. Her actions are motivated by the suicide of her best friend who was assaulted while attending a drunken party at college. The message in the movie is that men and onlookers claim innocence and point the finger of blame at the woman. The backdrop to the film is the patriarchy – but the lubricant for the action is alcohol.

Another relevant concept is social norms. In my mother's generation, the social norm was that nice girls didn't drink much. They certainly didn't get drunk. Having a drink meant having a small, sweet wine with Christmas dinner or a glass of sherry your husband ordered at the bar. Women didn't drink pints and any excess female drinking was something to be pitied and hidden. Not for one second am I saying this is preferable, but it was a social norm for her.

From the 1980s onwards, the social norm has been that young women drink as much as their male peers. Getting drunk is a laugh and getting tipsy at the kids' birthday party is okay. This dramatic change in what is seen as normal in society has had an impact on how we think, feel, and behave. Heavy drinking and even problem drinking is excused and dismissed. Even embarrassed friends will pass off a friend's drunken escapade as a bit of a lark or see it as letting off steam. We have become like fish in water – we don't even realize it is there. For many of us, a heavy drinking culture has become normal and acceptable.

Now, we can shake off the shackles of deception and we can choose freedom. Seeing alcohol as a release, or a route to relaxation, confidence, glamour, or freedom is part of the past. We now have true freedom to choose to drink – or not. We can establish a new social norm.

How Does Alcohol Affect Women?

When we stop drinking we may have regrets about how our drinking affected others – our families, friends, and loved ones. But perhaps the person harmed most is ourselves. Our bodies, minds, and emotions all take a bashing when we drink heavily, but how exactly does alcohol affect women?

Women absorb more alcohol and take longer to metabolize it. Although men are more likely to drink and imbibe more alcohol than women the effects of alcohol impact more dramatically on women. After drinking the same amount as men, women tend to have higher blood-alcohol levels than men, and the effects of alcohol happen more quickly and last longer.

These differences mean women are more vulnerable to long-term negative health consequences compared to men. Women are at risk of liver disease, cognitive decline, negative impacts on the heart, and cancers, especially breast cancer. These risks increase at lower levels of consumption than in men, and over fewer years.

(https://www.ncbi.nlm.nih.gov/pmc/articles/PMC316389 2/)

Women appear to be sensitive to the effects of alcohol due to fluctuating estrogen levels. When estrogen levels are low, as in perimenopause and post-menopause, alcohol can raise the levels of estrogen in the body. (https://integrativewomenshealthinstitute.com/alcohol-and-hormones/)

This rise in estrogen can intensify cravings. Many women who have been light drinkers have found that in mid-life their drinking becomes a problem. Empty nest syndrome and the emotional impact of children leaving home may be a cause of this new heavy drinking in older women, but the underlying cause could well be hormonal. Heavy alcohol consumption is correlated with an increased risk of breast cancer. In older women, heavy alcohol use increases the risk of osteoporosis, dementia, and heart disease. In younger women, drinking copiously can affect the ovaries affecting libido, hormones, and fertility.

Many of the women I have interacted with in research for this book have reported that their drinking has fluctuated over their lifetime and has increased in mid-life. A woman called Libby summed up her experience this way:

"My drinking progressed the older I got. I had a better job, more disposable income, and wine in the house all the time. I was able to work from home and cover up that I had been drinking all day as I was in a trusted position."

Libby's experience was echoed in the stories of countless women I spoke to.

The effects of alcohol on pregnant women and their babies are well documented and the latest advice in the UK and USA is that no level of alcohol consumption in pregnancy is deemed to be safe. In cases of heavy drinking, Alcohol Fetal Syndrome can affect the child for life. These facts have huge implications for the well-being of the child but also for the physical, emotional, and mental health of the mother. The stress, guilt, and shame of taking care of a child with Alcohol Fetal Syndrome can keep a woman locked into a downward spiral of self-reproach, regret, and depression. This is a heartbreaking situation. As a Social Worker, I worked with mothers in these situations, the unborn child is already on an 'at risk' register, and breaking out of this situation, which is often systemic, can be incredibly difficult.

Research has shown that women who experience depression are more likely to drink heavily. (https://www.healthline.com/health/mental-health/alcohol-and-depression) In many families, women are often the caregivers. In many cases, they take the lead in childcare, household organization, and the care of elderly or infirm relatives in the family. These caregiving roles can take their toll on women and lead to feelings of overwhelm, depression, and lack of life satisfaction; drinking alcohol can present itself as a solution. In addition, the constraints of women's roles also make it more difficult for women to get help if alcohol becomes a problem; women can find it difficult to get the support they need in terms of access to health, services, or peer support groups.

If you feel chronically sad, low, lethargic, guilty, worthless, or have suicidal thoughts, you might be self-medicating – using alcohol to feel better. All the alcohol is doing is numbing out the feelings and probably adding to the low mood as alcohol is a depressant. This struggle can be even more intense if there are added pressures such as difficulties with conceiving, having a child with special needs, a demanding job, or having peers who are not in the same situation.

Beth shared her experience with me in an email:

"I feel that the anxiety of being a full-time worker and a mum contributed, as alcohol was always used as a quick easy fix for stress. I had trouble conceiving and when I did get pregnant and everyone around me either had no desire for a family or had no trouble planning even the month, they wanted a child born. I drank to cover up my feelings about how this affected me. When I did have my son, I was looked down upon or so I thought for working full time and didn't have the social links enjoyed by other part-time or stay-at-home mums."

If you have felt very low for longer than a few weeks, and especially if you have thoughts of self-harm, get help. Talk to your doctor and reach out to others. Cutting out alcohol, or at least reducing it, will help – but you will need extra support to tackle a chronic low mood. Please make sure you get the support you need.

Research indicates that women are progressing much more quickly from heavy drinking to addiction. This is called telescoping. Telescoping is a term that describes a speeded-up progression from starting to drink, moving onto misuse, and progressing onto dependence. This journey appears to be an accelerated one for many women, especially younger women. The gender gap in telescoping between men and women has been closing quickly.

Abuse also plays a huge role in problem drinking. Females with PTSD are five times more likely to be alcohol-dependent than men. (https://www.nih.gov/news-events/news-releases/male-female-drinking-patterns-becoming-more-alike-us)

Sexual violence is a problem that needs to be tackled in its own right. Sadly, women who drink are at greater risk of sexual violence. I stress that in mentioning this *I am in no way blaming the woman who drinks*. Recent cases of female attacks and murders *without* alcohol present are a testament to the depressing reality, regardless of alcohol. Attacks, rapes, kidnappings, and murders *shouldn't* happen, but they do. Girls and women *should* be free to be out at any time, in any place, but sadly they are not. But the effects of drinking which include impaired reactions and reduced capacity to discern what is safe or unsafe can only make females more vulnerable in these situations. (https://www.cdc.gov/violenceprevention/sexualviolence /index.html).

In the US there are increasing community social policies that are bringing the number of attacks down and in the UK there have been recent efforts to tackle this problem systemically. These policy changes are absolutely what needs to happen, but the grim reality is that if a woman drinks, she is at increased risk of assault and rape. (https://www.gov.uk/government/news/foreign-secretary-launches-campaign-to-tackle-sexual-violence-in-conflict-around-the-world).

Earlier in the book, you will have read a chapter called 'Stop Beating Yourself Up' in which I talked about the importance of self-compassion. Eliminating problem drinking is probably the most compassionate and caring action you can take for yourself. By giving up heavy drinking you have stopped beating yourself up – physically, mentally, and emotionally. By stopping or at least reducing drinking you have taken huge steps in improving your health and well-being. The statistics show that you will be healthier and safer for putting the cork in the bottle.

FAQs.

Some general questions come up again and again when people are contemplating stopping drinking or are newly sober, so we will tackle them here. If you have another question not covered here, you can contact me via the contact page on winspress.com

"I can't stop drinking right away. Can I cut down and start the plan?"

Yes, absolutely. If you are drinking heavily and have signs of physical dependence it is unwise to completely stop suddenly. Signs of physical dependence are shaky hands, so-called' dry heaves' (feeling the strong urge to vomit with nothing coming up), sweating, anxiety, insomnia, and feeling the need to have an alcoholic drink in the morning or in the middle of the night to stave off nausea. If you experience these symptoms, it is safer to cut back gradually if you can. I would suggest cutting out one drink each day until you are down to a level you feel more comfortable with. You can still read this book and action what you can as you cut down.

"Should I moderate or abstain?"

This is a big question and will depend very much on personal drinking habits, level of concern, and long-term intentions. But you can ask yourself these few key questions that indicate that you need to abstain rather than moderate:

Have you tried many times to moderate but your resolve just disappears, and you break your own self-imposed rules? For example, have you decided in the morning you will not drink that day, but your intentions just dissolve by evening, and you go back to drinking?

The next question to ponder is when you drink, do seriously negative things happen like you get a DUI, or does your personality change dramatically? When you drink do you pick fights with people you care about or end up getting into trouble with the law and this happens again and again?

The third indication that you might need to completely abstain is if you are physically dependent on alcohol.

If you need to completely abstain, there is no shame in this. You could compare it to people who are sensitive to colorings or additives in food, if you avoid certain foods, there is no shame in that, so you can apply the same logic to alcohol.

Okay, so now let's go through some questions to ask yourself if you think you might be able to moderate. A good indicator that you could consider moderating is having a track record of being able to do this successfully. So, if you decide you will go to a party and just have two drinks and you can do this, not just once or twice but on most occasions, you have proved that you can drink moderately.

Sometimes people can drink moderately for years and then there is a huge negative life event, and their drinking has gone off the scale. Perhaps you have had a bereavement and you find yourself drinking heavily. If you have previously always drank moderately without negative consequences, you might well be able to return to this once you have dealt with the emotional upset. Finding other methods to soothe yourself and regain emotional equilibrium would be helpful.

Another question to ask yourself is: when I drink can I get along with people as usual and do I keep myself safe as I would if not drinking at all?

Of course, even if you think you can drink moderately, just because you *can* doesn't mean you *should.*

"Will I lose weight if I stop drinking?"

The answer to this depends on many personal factors. If women stop drinking and substitute alcohol with high-calorie foods in large amounts, any calorie deficit created by the lack of alcohol will be lost. So, if you stop and eat a mountain of chocolate every night, you certainly won't lose weight and you will probably put weight on.

Some drinkers, restrict food to allow for the calories in their alcohol. This means they stay slim but may well have vitamin and mineral deficiencies as alcohol does not contain any of these nutrients; it only has empty calories. So, when women who have this pattern of drinking stop, their weight probably won't change that much. They might well be eating more without the added calories from alcohol. Their calorie consumption levels off and of course, they will be healthier because they are ingesting more vitamins and minerals.

Bear in mind that alcohol is an appetite stimulant – hence aperitifs before meals. In addition, if you like to load up on a double cheeseburger and chips every night after a night's drinking, the resultant weight gain is not rocket science. So, if you have cleaned up your act and cut out the booze and the nightly cheeseburgers, you will probably lose weight.

One thing can be pretty much guaranteed, and that is if you stop drinking, you will most likely feel much more energetic. Perhaps not right away, give it a few weeks, but in time you will. This newfound energy will make you feel like moving more, dusting off the bike, or grabbing your unworn trainers, and you will be out there clocking up the miles.

As exercise has been proven to increase endorphins and all those feel-good chemicals, you will get addicted – in a good way – to moving your body regularly. For most people with average metabolisms, this will result in weight loss if needed, or easy weight maintenance.

I would urge you to take it easy. Give your body time to adjust, especially if you have been drinking heavily. If you need a little sugar to help you get over the worst in the first few days or weeks, just go with it – in moderation. Look at this as a transition. It would be best to avoid starting a restrictive diet at the same time as stopping drinking. It won't work, and you might well end up drinking again, so easy does it. Focus on eating a range of foods for good health and nutrition.

Above all, give yourself time and your weight will most likely level off if it needs to. If you are having issues with this, speak with your healthcare professional.

"I've read that a glass of red wine a day is good for you. Is this true?"

A famous doctor has said: ''People love to hear good news about their bad habits.'' And this old chestnut concerning red wine falls into that category. Red wine contains a chemical component called resveratrol, which gives it its dark hue. Research indicates that resveratrol does have some benefits for heart health, but you can get resveratrol in red grape juice without the negative health impacts of alcohol.

Also, these studies recommend extremely low amounts – a small glass once a day. Some people can have a small glass once a day, but many can't. If you can't stick to a very moderate amount, then excess alcohol will cancel out any benefits gained from the resveratrol in the red wine.

"Do I need to do a medical detox?"

That depends on how much you have been drinking and whether you are physically addicted. If you cannot go 24 hours without a drink, you might need a medically supervised detox. If in doubt, speak to your doctor.

"What about AA? Does it work for women?"

Lana shared the following with me via email in response to an *Alcohol Recovery Show* podcast episode:

"I went to AA for a few weeks. They were half female half male, and the people were great. The program didn't suit me though. I was encouraged to read the Big Book – the section on women was awful. It's all about how a housewife treats her recovering husband. The people in the group said to ignore it and just take on board the message, but as a career woman I just couldn't."

Laura's summary of her experience touches on issues raised by many women. AA has and does work for millions of women over decades. If you are attracted to AA, I would encourage you to attend a meeting and decide for yourself. However, women can be put off by the initial experiences of reading the 'Big Book' or attending a few meetings. But there is much more to AA than initial impressions, such as Laura's would suggest.

I would also say that change is easier from the inside. Being part of AA and highlighting these issues will be more effective than external criticism after one meeting or two, so give it a go if it appeals to you and then decide. I discuss AA more in the section that deals with the question, *Am I an Alcoholic?*

"How can I have fun/relax/celebrate without a drink?"

There are lots of ideas in this book to answer that question. Once you stop drinking and feel more energetic, not to mention free up more time and money by not drinking, you will wonder how you ever found the time to drink!

"Can I stop drinking on my own?"

It is possible, but staying stopped for the long term can be difficult if you try to do so without support. This book is about putting together a method that works for you, so you will find lots of ideas on building a support system that works for you. These could be formal programs of recovery, or they could just be making sure you have a few sober-sympathetic friends to support you in your efforts in an informal way. I would urge you not to try to do it alone. Making connections with others ensure you are not only getting support, but you are accountable. Knowing that you have told friends you have stopped drinking might make you think twice before lifting a drink again.

"What sort of drinks can I drink if I want to avoid alcohol?"

There are lots of ideas on the WinsPress website. I have put together a free guide to non-alcoholic drinks. You can find it under the 'Free Stuff' tab at winspress.com.

"I am worried about my sister's drinking. What can I do to get her to stop?"

Sadly, it is impossible to get someone to stop if they are not ready to face the issue. You could share your own experience with her and pass on this book to her. Hopefully, you will sow some seeds that will take root when she is ready.

"I can stop drinking for a while, but I hit it hard again when I feel low or have too much time on my hands. What can I do to stop?"

Re-read this book and follow The Plan. It will help you to cope with triggers such as stress, boredom, or low mood and help prepare you for the risk of relapse.

"I am finding it hard to stop drinking or even cut down. Is there any medication that might help me?"

I have a free podcast called *The Alcohol Recovery Show* and in Episode 15, my partner at WinsPress, addictions therapist Lewis David, presents the most common medications used to help people stop drinking. Medications are not a magic bullet and counseling, and social support is recommended alongside medication. You can find *The Alcohol Recovery Show* at winspress.com/podcast and on most major podcast platforms.

"*I find it very difficult to resist cravings to drink. What can I do?*"

Follow the suggestions in this book on how to deal with cravings. Also, you will find free resources on the winspress.com website, such as the free 'Urge Surfing Meditation' that will help you overcome cravings. And try listening to *The Alcohol Recovery Show* when cravings are a problem.

"*I don't know if I am addicted to alcohol. I just know I drink a lot most days, what are the signs of addiction?*"

Dependency on alcohol is characterized by an inability to abstain from alcohol, difficulty in controlling behavior around alcohol, feeling physically ill when you abstain from drinking, obsessing about drinking or getting a drink, and trying to diminish the severity of the problem.

Another common question is: 'Am I an alcoholic?' I address this in the next chapter.

Am I an Alcoholic?

This question can drive people nuts. It is a testament to the taboo and moral judgment that society has placed around issues with alcohol that this has happened. After all, no one tries to prove they are not diabetic or arthritic. The question "Am I an alcoholic?" can be contentious in the world of recovery. People can get upset if this is questioned.

People can get tied up in knots about this, so to lighten what can be a heavy topic, I would like to share a true story with you.

A friend of mine recounted an experience on a recent trip to Italy. Mary is an Irish lady, who attends AA and has about 18 years of continuous sobriety. She was very conscientious about attending meetings and whilst on holiday she enquired about AA meetings at the hotel reception. The receptionist wrote down a name and address close to the hotel and told Mary to enquire there.

Mary duly trotted off to find the building close by and buzzed at the door of the address she was given. She was led into an office and greeted warmly by an Italian man in a white coat. He appraised her in a slightly puzzled way and inquired when she had last had an alcoholic drink. "Eighteen years ago," Mary replied brightly. The confused expression on the Italian's face deepened. "Why are you here?" he asked. Mary explained and the confusion cleared.

I share this story to illustrate the dual interpretation of the word 'alcoholic.' In the medical world, it means someone who is currently physically addicted to alcohol. In the minds of the general population, it probably means something similar: someone who drinks in the morning and foregoes food, companionship, family, occupation, and other meaningful activities in life to get alcohol. The ubiquitous person in a dirty trench coat with a bottle in the pocket on a park bench. This stereotype is unfortunate. Its negative moral and social overtones can stop people from getting help whether they are an alcoholic or not.

Like my friend Mary, millions of people refer to themselves as alcoholics even though it has been months, years, or decades since they drank. Many people find it a relief to finally realize what the problem is. They are not mad or bad, they accept they are an alcoholic. The label goes beyond the medical definition based on a physiological state and sums up a set of personality traits, thinking, and psychological quirks that makes someone an alcoholic in AA. I once heard it said that "You are safer pretending to be an alcoholic in AA than pretending you are not an alcoholic outside." For many people, admitting defeat and declaring themselves an alcoholic is a huge relief, but for others, the label just does not sit comfortably. They have had problems with drinking but cannot bring themselves to apply the label to themselves. In AA speak this can drive people to insanity and death. Some people will call this denial. But what about the people who recognize they have an issue with drinking but cannot bring themselves to refer to themselves as an alcoholic?

In the world of professional recovery, no one is referred to as an alcoholic. In the medical and social work field, labels that define a person by their condition are discouraged. For example, in the UK the term 'deaf-mute' would be unacceptable. The term used would be a 'person with a hearing impairment and no speech'. It is respectful and acknowledges a person's dignity as a human being *before* the condition.

The same logic could be applied to the term alcoholic. In public health, a person with valid concerns about their drinking could be referred to as a person with an alcohol use disorder. This puts the person first and not the label. Many people feel more comfortable with this and will adhere to a program of recovery using this term.

In AA there are a set of questions to work through to decide if you are an alcoholic. No one else but you apply the label. No one diagnoses you. You decide. If you work through the questions and you find it helpful to acknowledge the answers are yes to most of the questions and the program appeals, this can be a massive step forward. The problem is acknowledged, and you have found a solution. So, stick with it.

In AA terms asking, "Am I an alcoholic?" is a question only you can answer.

What is clear is that if you have had serious, repeated unwanted, and negative consequences of drinking, it is probably not safe to drink again whatever label you do or do not apply to yourself. So, it might be more useful to ask yourself "Can I drink without bad things happening? Can I truly take it or leave it? Do I crave alcohol or worry if I can't get it? Do I obsess over it? Do I set a limit on my drinking and then go over it?"

So, to summarise: The term 'alcoholic' is not currently favored by professionals in the field of alcohol recovery. It is considered a rather old-fashioned label, heavy with connotations of shame and 'otherness.' Instead, it is considered more helpful to think of issues with drinking or the misuse of alcohol as being on a type of spectrum or sliding scale.

If you imagine a scale that on one end has the type of person who doesn't enjoy drinking at all or might have one small sherry once a year at Christmas and on the other extreme of the scale, there is the person who is physically dependent on alcohol, for example, someone who needs to drink to get rid of the shakes or is at risk of seizure if they don't keep topping up with alcohol. Along this scale is all manner of people with different levels of dependence, habits, or issues.

What's more, these issues can increase or decrease in seriousness or severity over time or in different circumstances. You might be further along than some other folk or further back towards the light drinker. In modern professional alcohol recovery circles, medical personnel and therapists will use the term *Alcohol Use Disorder* (AUD for short). This covers a range of people with concerns about their drinking.

At WinsPress we have a questionnaire you can use to work out if you would meet the criteria of AUD. This questionnaire has helped clarify this question for thousands of people. If you would like a copy of the questionnaire, you can get a downloadable PDF version free from www.subscribepage/free-pdf.

Another common question concerns Alcoholics Anonymous. Women trying to get sober may consider attending but dismiss it because they do not want to label themselves as an alcoholic. Members of Alcoholics Anonymous will use the term 'alcoholic' to introduce themselves in a meeting. But labeling yourself an alcoholic is not a pre-requisite for membership of the fellowship. To be a member you must simply 'have a *desire* to stop drinking'. It is an abstinence-based program. If you want to go to a meeting to see what happens there, you can do so. You do not have to introduce yourself as an alcoholic. If it is your turn to speak just say 'pass'. If you want to say something to the group you can introduce yourself as a newcomer or 'a grateful member of the fellowship' or simply just say your name if you want to. Some people at the meeting might raise an eyebrow. This is because the members are urged to label themselves as an alcoholic to instill a sense of humility and remind themselves of what they are. This works for some people and not others.

As I have said, no one in AA no one will tell you that you are an alcoholic, but you are encouraged to ask yourself certain questions about whether you are, and you decide for yourself. AA has helped millions to get well and maintain sobriety, so give it a go, if you are attracted to it. Attend a few meetings and decide for yourself. In many areas, there are women-only meetings, so this type of meeting might be a more comfortable one in which to get started in AA if that's what you feel led to do.

Many of the women I spoke to were put off AA – some attended meetings where there were more men than women. You might not be put off by that but if you are going to some different meetings. You will find one where there is a more equal balance of men and women.

Reading the main text of AA – commonly referred to as the 'Big Book' – can be off-putting, especially the chapter 'To Wives' which comes across as outdated and sexist. It was written in the later 1930s when society was very different so it will seem old-fashioned. However, do keep an open mind and keep going if you find the meetings and the program helpful. The best way to change an organization (although AA states it is a fellowship and not an organization) is from the inside, so keep up the female presence and push for change.

Closing Thoughts.

A huge thank you to all the women who have generously shared experiences, hopes, and encouragement. The book is written to acknowledge the needs women have in recovery – the need to grow feelings of self-confidence and self-esteem, and how to shake off guilt, shame, and humiliation.

I have interviewed and exchanged emails and messages with countless women from a range of backgrounds in researching for this book. I hope that all women reading it will find it relatable and honor their experiences. In addition, I have worked as a social worker and teacher for thirty years across four countries and two continents. The contexts have varied from inner cities to rural villages and from private settings to state provisions. I have also drawn on my experiences in these diverse settings.

By writing a book for women the last thing I want to do is reinforce stereotypes, but I do write based on my own experience and that of women I have worked with. Also with female readers and podcast listeners who have interacted with me to help with this book. So what I have written about reflects these experiences.

In my younger days, the word 'sober' sounded dry, dull, and cold. I believe now that I had absorbed messages from the situation I grew up in that reinforced these notions. So, if sobriety was dull, drinking was exciting, vibrant, and cheerful. But I guess if you picked up this book, drinking has stopped being a positive experience. A basic belief we need to reconfigure is that drinking is all fun and frolic. It can be, for a while but think about the cost: health problems, relationship issues, job difficulties, and more. If drinking is costing you more than money, it's time to redefine beliefs around sobriety. I hope this book has helped you do that.

To be alcohol-free, all we need to do is not drink. That's all. That's the price tag.

What do we get in return? Where shall I start? The benefits are limitless: improved energy levels, sleep, relationships, productivity, self-regard, positivity, finances, mood, memory, ability to relax naturally, empathy, mental clarity, and feeling comfortable in our skin. I hope that if you have stopped drinking you are beginning to feel some of the benefits. If you are still drinking, perhaps try going alcohol-free for a few weeks and see how you feel.

This book is called 'The Alcohol-Free Woman' because I truly believe being sober is the gateway to authentic freedom. No one is asking you to *give up* drinking, you are being encouraged and guided in *letting go* of drinking. In making efforts to get sober and recover from the effects alcohol has had on your life, you are choosing to be free.

So, see sobriety as a huge get-out-of-jail card. You will be free to find out who you are, what makes you tick, and who you want to be. See sobriety as a big adventure in finding out more about yourself and the world you live in.

When we are drinking our thinking and our world become smaller. Many women share with me how their drinking escalated, and their lives became centered around the sofa and the wine bottle. For many, it became a lonely and sad existence. For others who were out on the party scene, their lives were curtailed. For example, Shauna shared her experience with me:

"In my twenties, I went out a lot. I found it hard to sit in for an evening. I avoided activities where I couldn't get a drink, like going to the cinema or exercising. I lived in a flat close to town so I could get to pubs and bars easily, my vacations and trips were to places where I could get alcohol and I never had the mental energy to learn anything new. Once I left college, my energies were focused on working my job and drinking. That was it. Seems boring when I look at it like that."

Perhaps you have drunk to deal with difficult emotions, anxiety, trauma, or just a daily low-level feeling of depression. You don't need me to point out that drinking might take the edge off, but the edge always comes back sharper. Drinking is not a long-term solution. Instead see sobriety as the happy, safe space you can create for yourself.

You don't need to escape into a fog of alcohol-induced lethargy. You can wake up and enjoy all the benefits of an alcohol-free recovery. Those benefits will include less anxiety, depression, and difficult emotions. In addition, by being alcohol-free you will develop the skills and identify the resources you have available in your life to tackle the individual challenges you have. But you don't have to take it from me. Try it for yourself as an experiment and see how you feel.

Making any change, especially sustainable change takes vision, intention, skills, and resources. I hope that this 9-point plan has helped you find your vision and intention, develop the skills and identify the resources in your life to become an alcohol-free woman.

Lastly, I am told that the number 9 signifies the end of one cycle and the beginning of another. It is about personal growth and development. It is my sincere hope that this new cycle is one in which you thrive. I wish you abundance and happiness in all that you do – alcohol-free.

***

Thank you for reading my book.

I would be immensely grateful if you could leave a review on Amazon.

Printed in Great Britain
by Amazon

12109519R00157